Tie Me Up
with Rainbows

A guide to beauty and color
for you and your home.

By Bernice Kentner
Author of
"COLOR ME A SEASON"

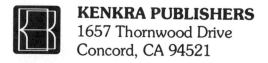

KENKRA PUBLISHERS
1657 Thornwood Drive
Concord, CA 94521

ISBN 0-941522-02-4

A KEN-KRA Publication

1657 Thornwood Drive
Concord, California
94521

TX 788 156

Booklets Printed 1980
First Printing 1982
Second Printing 1984

This publication has been written and dedicated to all those who know and love their Season and who want to make the most of their God given color design.

Many thanks to our Color Me A Season Model Nora Jackman for posing for the cover and to Stephen Krause for illustrations.

FOREWORD

I have been very grateful for the response to my publications on color. I wanted to make the purchase of the individual booklets easier for you, so we have combined the following publications into one volume.

CONTOURING THE FACE WITH COLOR
FASHION LINE AND DESIGN
YOUR CROWNING GLORY
COLOR, ITS EFFECT ON YOU AND OTHERS
INTERIOR DESIGN FOR YOU AND YOUR SEASON

The booklet "Understanding Yourself and Others" has been included completely in the book A RAINBOW IN YOUR EYES and so it has not been printed in this compilation.

As in nature, rainbows usually follow a storm. Our beauty with color doesn't just happen—it does take a little more than just knowing your colors to choose your clothing from and purchase some beautiful cosmetics for your face. As a painter prepares his pallet for his picture, we also need to have a lovely complexion to apply our colors of cosmetics on.

Hair that is beautiful and in perfect style for us is important to the final picture and, if perchance, you, like myself have a figure a little less than perfect, it is good to know some camouflage techniques with color that will make us into the lovely creatures that we all want to be.

Color makes us happy and our surroundings are important to us. The interior design portion is important not only to our feelings but also to how we look in our color background.

I have tried to impart some of my training as a cosmetologist and a color analyst in this book in what I hope will be a practical and helpful instruction manual on beauty and color.

Bernice Kentner

TABLE OF CONTENTS

CONTOURING THE FACE WITH SEASONS' LIGHTS AND COLOR GLOW

Includes Skin Care for a
More Beautiful Complexion

Your body has a color that identifies YOU. You are an important person. You matter to others. The way you look affects people around you. The colors you wear either blend or fight with what we call your Season (your personal color design).

This booklet has additional information to help you know more about enhancing your Season by improving your complexion and using color to camoflauge flaws on that otherwise beautiful face. There are very few flawless beauties but you are about to become one—at least it will seem so.

Since you are reading this booklet I assume you have previ-

1

ously read **"Color Me A Season"** . . . How to find and use your most flattering colors. If you have not read it I hope you will try to obtain a copy. It will be necessary to know what your Season is to understand the colors we will be putting on your face in the contouring portion.

The skin of the body is the canvas upon which we will place color to enhance your beauty. The smoother and more flawless it is, the more refined the final picture will be.

Have you ever tried to paint a picture on a rough surface? As a child did you ever try to do your homework on a nubby, oilcloth covered table? It is impossible to have a smooth finished project. We must therefore begin our project by making the face as blemish free as possible.

WHAT IS YOUR SKIN TYPE?

Many things affect the complexion; weather, age, health, diet, cleansing habits, etc. Some skin types are inherited just as your Season is. Some families have blemished skin and others do not. We will do the most we can to help you improve your complexion and try to camouflage those we cannot do anything about.

NORMAL SKIN

If you have to ask yourself if your complexion is dry or oily you probably have what we call normal skin type. If there are no particular problems, you can consider yourself in the normal range. Even if you have a few blemishes, once or twice a month, you are still in that category.

DRY SKIN

The surface of the skin will feel dry and chapped, not just after washing but most of the time. It may have red blotches and have a dull coarse appearance. In severe cases actual cracks may appear on the surface of the skin.

2

OILY SKIN

Your hair gives a real clue to your skin type. If it is extremely oily, your skin may be also. If your forehead, nose or skin is shiny after a thorough cleansing you may be sure you fall in the oily range.

COMBINATION SKIN

It is possible to have dry areas on the skin and oily in other areas. Over-treating of one or the other will leave problems and each area should be treated for its particular type.

In our skin care program we will consider the different areas of cleansing for your particular complexion.

The way we treat our skin during the day is actually a part of skin care. Over-exposure to the sun or elements can only dry out or irritate the skin's surface. Day after day treatment like this will cause the skin to age.

Bad health and diet will contribute to a lackluster skin.

The largest organ of the body, our skin, reflects what we put into the body as well as what is eliminated. Irregularity of the body in any way may show up on the skin's surface.

POOR FOOD CHOICES

Getting enough sleep and proper food and exercise will show up in your complexion. It is worth the effort to care for yourself as well as your skin.

BLEMISHES

Before getting into our skin care, we need to consider those pesky breaking out spots on the face. Lucky you if they are the kind that form pustules that may be opened with a sterilized needle and removed by gentle pressure. You are not lucky that you have them, but fortunate that at least they come to a head and go away with proper care.

A great many women over thirty are bothered with blemishes that are actually cysts that will not come to a head and are difficult to remove because there seems to be no core or cause. A cyst is a skin pore that becomes infected but has no opening by which the plug or offending cause can be removed. Sometimes it can swell to tremendous proportions and weep with a yellow-like fluid. This must be treated by a dermatologist who might prescribe cortisone salves and antibiotics.

Tetracycline is the most common cure for infected skin. It works well to clear up acne and cysts. It does have some side effects but it should be considered by you and your doctor for serious skin infections.

Whiteheads are gatherings of oil in an openless pore. They too have no pore opening and must be removed with a sterilized needle. The skin over a whitehead is usually quite tough and hard to penetrate into the actual oil deposit. I insert the needle and then gently twist the needle working into the center of the pore. When the surface of the pore and the inner part of the oil deposit are opened then you may remove the blemish with firm pressure. Use the same precautions for opening blackheads to keep from scarring the skin. (Use tissue or soft cloth to cover the tips of the fingers when pressing the skin to remove either blackheads or whiteheads.)

Red blemishes that itch or just weep may be allergies; probably to something that has been placed on the skin. It may also come from something you have eaten.

Areas that are red and irritated may be infected oil glands. It may be necessary to see a good dermatologist for any kind of infection or spotting that cannot be treated or removed after a reasonable time.

It seems an added expense to see a specialist, but one visit to a qualified physician can solve a problem that a general practitioner cannot do. Be sure to take the medication and follow your doctor's directions until your skin is back to normal. Go easy on returning to creams and lotions. Try one thing at a time to be sure you can tolerate it.

CLEANSING ROUTINE

It is important to keep the complexion immaculately clean, allowing it to secrete its natural oils and yet cleansing it thoroughly morning and night.

Every time we cleanse the skin it removes oil and what is sometimes called the acid mantle of the skin. I feel the skin returns to its own normal balance as the oil glands secrete and replace the oil washed away. Too much cleansing can be irritating to the balance of the skin.

We must use intelligence with skin care. I have seen oily complexions that ooze more oil after cleansing and scrubbing with

soap because the oil glands in the skin are irritated by harsh cleansers. At first the skin feels very clean but soon is oozing with more oil than ever.

I have had somewhat normal skin during my lifetime and as a young girl I washed my face with any kind of soap available. I soon found that this was making me have a very oily nose and chin. When introduced to a skin care line that used a cleansing cream I felt sure that this would add to my oil problems. Amazingly enough, soon after starting a cleansing routine with a less harsh cleanser than soap, I found my oil problems were solved.

Before going into cleansing routines I want to make sure you know that excess handling or touching of the face may add to oil and blemish problems of the skin. It is important after cleansing our face to forget about it and not pick at blemishes, etc. There will be special care times (explained later) that will take care of problem areas but try to remember to keep your hands off your face as much as possible.

Another thing that adds to blemish problems is unclean hair. Those who are broken out on the forehead often style their hair in some sort of way to help cover that area. If hair is not kept immaculately clean it can add to the complexion problem.

WHEN TO CLEANSE

It should be fairly obvious that we need to clean our faces at night, but countless women and girls go to bed without cleansing their faces. This is the most important time to get off all the daytime soil and stale secretions of the skin.

Faces press against pillows and soil can enter the pores. This is a perfect time for the beauty treatment of sleep and rest. The skin should be clean and ready for a deserved rest.

WHAT TO USE

I feel a cleanser that is water removable is perfect for the cleansing program. A cleansing creme in lotion form or a gentle jar cleanser creme is compatible to all types of complexions. They are formulated to dissolve dirt and grime and to be removed with a warm, wet, nubby washcloth.

For very oily complexions I recommend a second step in cleansing by washing the face with a gentle complexion soap.

First apply the cleansing lotion over the entire face and throat. Rub in upward motions all over the face. Do not be afraid to scrub with the pads of the fingers because dead skin cells are always on the surface of the skin and need to be removed.

Using the washcloth that is warm, not hot, wash the creamy cleanser off the face. Go behind your ears and back of neck too with the washcloth. (When bathing, remember to scrub the hairline area on the back of the neck, the ears, and behind the ears with regular bath soap, but do not wash your face with regular soap.)

Rinse the cloth out at least three times and remove every trace of cleanser and soil.

SPECIAL TREATMENTS

Once or twice a week you will want to use either *Honey and Almond Scrub* (for normal and dry types) or *T-Zone Scrub* (formulated with ingredients to help dry up oil) for oily complexions.

When using *Honey and Almond Scrub,* wet the fingers and apply about one teaspoon of the scrub and gently scrub the skin of the face. Work in circular upward motions and concentrate on areas that have blackheads and crusty skin. Two or three minutes will be sufficient to remove some of the dead skin off the face. (Caution—if your skin is easily irritated, or has an oil gland infection, skip any scrub. Use only the cleanser or complexion bar. Follow directions from your dermatologist until he has your skin problems corrected.)

T-Zone Scrub will help remove oil from your skin. Use it two or three times a week. You will really notice a difference with this product. The fine granules reach into the pores and help unplug them.

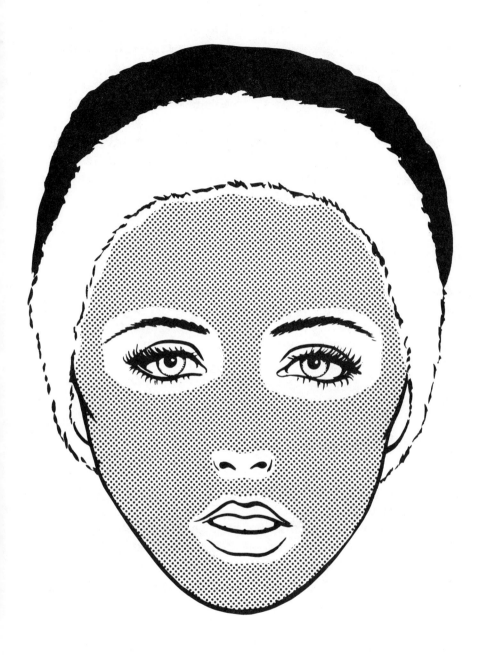

On days that you do not use the scrub, choose one to do a
Spearmint Masque. Apply about a teaspoon all over the face,
avoiding the eye area, and allow to dry for fifteen minutes. This is

9

an excellent toning masque and will help to draw out impurities. Use *Spearmint Masque* on blemishes anytime you have a breakout. Apply a small amount on the blemish and wash off with water in the morning. This really helps to draw out and dry up pimples.

Our second step in skin cleansing for oily skin is to lather up the *Complexion Bar* and wash the face, concentrating on the oily areas only. Before I would go to this step of cleansing I would give the *Milky Cleanser* a chance to work for about a month to see if oil glands will subside their production of excess oil. If not, then go to the *Complexion Bar* (step two) and *T-Zone Scrub* for special treatment times.

Now tone the skin with *Skin Toning Lotion.* Apply a small amount of toner on a cotton ball immediately after using the wet wash cloth. Wipe gently over the face but with firm enough pressure to remove any remaining soil. Toner will reach down into the pores and get the oil and dirt missed by cleanser and soaps. It will tone the complexion by working up the circulation of the blood supply. It should make your face tingle. Avoid going too close to the eye areas.

RESTORING SKIN BALANCE

Before retiring for the night and immediately after using moisture on the face with water or toner, you should treat the skin to a night cream.

Richer night creams are especially helpful for overly dry skin. They should be applied sparingly to the face. The small amount should absorb immediately into the skin and there will be less chance to leave residue of oils on your pillowcase and bedding.

For extremely dry skin types this rich night cream is very helpful. They usually contain lanolin, obtained from animal sources. This has a special softening effect and is most like the oil in human skin. You may even feel the need of both types for the night time treatment. don't overdo it, but use enough to thoroughly cover your complexion. Skin will absorb all it can in twenty minutes.

Moisture creme should be applied to all types of skin if you don't need the richer creams. If your face is oily on your nose and forehead, use the moisturizer on the areas of the face that do not have an over oily problem.

For normal complexions, apply a fine film of moisture cream over the entire face and down on the throat area.

Moisturizers are important because they help hold water in the skin. They are important at night especially because the pillowcase and bedding pressed against the face can remove moisture that your skin produces. Most homes do not have enough moisture in the air, especially in winter time when heaters are on.

MORNING CLEANSING ROUTINE

After all that cleansing in the evening one would think it unnecessary to cleanse again in the morning, but consider the elements in the air that you have come in contact with. Even lying on the pillow has added some lint and fibers, plus the air contains dust particles that settle on everything during the night, including your face. Oil has secreted from the oil glands in a natural way and just everything has added to the necessity to cleanse again quickly in the morning.

Upon arising, those with normal to dry complexions will want to quickly run a warm (not hot) washcloth over the face without any soaps or cleansers. Letting the water from the shower run on your face and massaging with fingertips is also a good idea.

We add moisture to the skin all over the body in bath and shower. Moisture is the one element we want to capture in our cleansing routine. That is why it is important to apply moisturizer right after cleansing with water.

Skin Toning Lotion also contains moisture and this is the second step to the morning cleansing. A cotton ball saturated with the toner quickly applied to the face will not only add moisture and tone, it will help wake you up in the morning. The coolness of the toner causes the pores to retract and closes the pores to some extent.

11

Those of you who have large troublesome pores may want to do one of two things. Instead of applying toner in the morning you may use an astringent. An astringent contains aluminum salts. It may be called an astringent, but without the alum it will only be a toner.

The aluminum salts, or zinc salts, cause the skin around the pore opening to swell or puff up hiding the pore for several hours.

If your skin toner does not close pores well, simply apply one-half teaspoon Alum from the spice rack and shake until dissolved. Ice cold water will also close the pores but not for a long period of time.

WHEN TO USE AN ASTRINGENT

Unless the pores of your skin are extremely stretched, I would use the regular toner. If you can take the head of a straight pin and fit it into some of your skin pores, then you have a problem and need the astringent. One reason you need to close them is to eliminate dirt and debris that combines with the oil in the pore to cause a plug or blackhead. Often those with large pores have blackheads because the skin is open to soil, makeup, etc.

When closing the pores we find that the cosmetics used will not enter the pore openings. We are preparing the skin as a painter's canvas and we want to do all we can to make it smoother and beautiful.

MOISTURIZING

Immediately after the astringent or toner, we need to apply a small amount of a good moisture creme. A little goes a long way and we only want to put a fine film over the cleansed and moistened skin. A moisturizer seals in moisture better than some oils. The pores can still secrete and the skin around the pores will retain moisture.

When I took my cosmetology training it was thought that the one cure for wrinkles was a rich oily cream. Women loaded their skin down at night with these rich-in-oil concoctions but still the complexion wrinkled; probably a little slower because the oils

WATER

would to some extent stop the evaporation. At the same time they added, to those with normal to oily skin, problems of excess oil on the upper dead cell area.

In recent years we have learned something from food dehydration. Take a little raisin for instance and soak it in water to plump it up. It will still be darkened and lined but adding water takes it back up to original size. Reverse process . . . set a green grape out in the sun with no protection and within hours it will dry and wrinkle up. If we put a coating of food oil round it and let it stand it will take longer and the surface will be smooth, but the underneath dries up and loses shape and form. Now plop another little fresh grape into a jar of water and it will stay fresh for days.

YOU SUN LOVERS TAKE A LESSON HERE!

After the moisturizing, makeup *foundation* should be applied immediately. Many women argue about using a foundation and feel it is harmful to the skin or too made-up looking. They feel it is unnatural.

I like to use a moistened sponge to apply foundation. A good foundation is usually water based with just enough oil in it to add a glow. Those products which are completely water based, or natural as some like to claim, will dry like a powder on the skin. Oil added to a foundation is usually mineral oil. Fewer people are allergic to it.

13

A WORD ABOUT NATURAL COSMETICS

Did you know that any cosmetic can be called *natural* according to the food and drug laws if it contains at least one or more substance which was originally a living thing. Hence, just about any cosmetic could be termed natural.

If you are a person who has problems with cosmetic allergies it will more than likely be to either lanolin or a fragrance added.

It may make you feel better if your cosmetic says natural, but most of us would be better off using a cosmetic chosen for its non-allergenic properties.

BACK TO FOUNDATION APPLICATION

Apply the foundation on the sponge. About three times tipping the bottle will cover most faces. We do not put foundation on the throat area but work it in under the chin so there is no line of demarcation.

If there are areas that have spots of discoloration you may apply directly from the bottle in these areas. This will give you better coverage. You may not want to use the sponge and that is alright also; just moisten your fingertips as you work with it.

This is where you will find a difference in foundations. Usually those of cheaper quality will be runnier because they have been diluted down with water.

WHY A FINE FILM OF FOUNDATION?

Putting on foundation with water lets your Season's coloring shine through. It feels better and takes away the mask effect.

Those over thirty must be especially careful about thick foundation coverage or cream base covers. The skin begins to take on *character* lines. A very thick foundation will show up every line or crease on our skin's canvas.

I hate to keep picking on that magical age thirty, but the bloom does begin to fade a little then.

There seems to be a tendency with girls before marriage or about twenty to use every beauty concoction on the market trying

14

to find their image. Then after marriage too many fall into that category of not enough time to use makeup or care for the skin.

I believe women owe it to themselves and others to keep that fresh glow of youth as long as possible. Men, after all, spend time shaving and grooming themselves every day. Is it too much for a woman to spend ten minutes in the morning and evening for a beauty routine?

In my experience I have found it is those women who have worked at keeping their skin wrinkle free who look better at fifty.

TO PICK OR NOT TO PICK

I know some of you are wondering what to do with black-heads, pimples, pustules, and cysts. Most beauty books tell you to leave your hands off them.

I personally cannot stand seeing a blemish that is white and ready to open just sitting there on someone's face needing attention. I feel it is important to learn about caring for these things. If properly done you can remove them yourself.

Blackheads —

Steam the face with a hot but tolerable washcloth for

15

about ten minutes. This opens the pores. Wrap a piece of cloth around your fingertips and placing the fingers on each side of the blackhead apply gentle pressure to remove the plug. Do this very carefully or you will scrape the skin and wind up with a scab on your face that takes time to heal.

Some pores close when you press towards them making it almost impossible to open a blackhead. In this case you will need a suction type instrument for blackhead removal (follow directions on the box or instruction sheet, how to use).   Remove as many of the blackheads as you can without overworking the skin.

When you are done with your treatment, rinse your cloth in very cool water to close the pores. Tone the skin with *Skin Toning Lotion*. Be careful for some time after this treatment to keep those areas especially clean because the pores have been stretched with oil plugs and will be open to soil, etc.

Whiteheads —

Before steaming the face, the whitehead must be punctured with a sterilized needle. Very gently try to break through into the inner core of the clogged pore.

Steam the area for a few minutes with very warm water. With your fingertips covered with cloth, push gently on all sides of the whitehead until it comes out. If you cannot remove it you will have to puncture deeper into the center of the pore. After removal, splash cold water on the area and swab with *Skin Toning Lotion*.

For rashes, broken blood vessels, and cysts, see your dermatologist. Do not delay because medication is available for such conditions before the skin becomes permanently scarred.

We have now removed the skin problems (hopefully) and your complexion can begin to improve.

CLEANING THE FACE OF UNWANTED FACIAL HAIR

Before we can proceed with the actual cosmetic application,

we must inspect the face for hairs that will interfere with facial beauty. Sometimes we neglect this little touch of good grooming.

Do you have any hairs growing out of facial moles? Ask your doctor about removing these hairs by tweezing. In the meantime keep them cut off.

Look at your face closely (in a magnifying mirror if needs be) to see if you have hair growing out of the nostrils, around the mouth or in the brow area.

Tweezing the eyebrows may not be pleasant, but unless you arch your brows properly you destroy the framing of the eye. It is practically impossible to apply a highlighter under the brow when hair is present. Hints on tweezing the brows and how to do it are on page 81 in **"Your Crowning Glory,"** Hair care and styling for your Season.

DO YOU REALLY NEED A FACE LIFT?

Character lines and wrinkles come over the years from stretched skin. We can do a lot with face contouring to alleviate the problem. We want to be as youthful as possible but most of us do not NEED a face lift.

Keeping weight down is one way to keep the skin in an unstretched condition. If you have recently lost a great deal of weight you will notice a lot of looseness on the face. A lot of it will tone up especially if it was a fast weight loss. You probably do not need face surgery.

Smoking really causes fast wrinkling of the skin. Your cigarette could be called a face dehydrator as the warm smoke constantly rises up over it. The squinting of the eyes as you smoke doesn't do a great deal for crows-feet either.

Facial surgery is very costly and you should be sure you are not just trying to capture your lost youth. Aging can be very beautiful you know!

When sagging eyelids interfere with the way you see, etc., then facial surgery should be considered. I also feel that when a person has an extremely ugly nose structure or face deformity no cost should be spared to repair that condition. Thousands of

17

dollars are spent yearly for straightening teeth on children. If a facial feature causes great concern and embarrassment for a child, it should be corrected, too.

Your profession also might cause you to consider facial cosmetic surgery. Those in show business who depend on their face for their fortune should by all means do what they can to protect their livelihood. There are probably others who, because of their necessity to retain a youthful apearance, should consider it also. I would, on the whole, consider aging as one of the beautiful stages of life. I don't think older women are any less beautiful than the young. They are beautiful in a different way. Beauty can be enhanced for women of all ages and I will continue now to show you how to do it.

CONTOURING WITH SEASONS' LIGHTS AND COLOR GLOW

We have studied how to cleanse and care for the skin to prepare it for contouring. We have applied foundation and now our painting canvas is ready.

COVER UP CREAM LIGHTENER

Use a cover up cream to contour the face and make it look younger.

On the face diagram you will see that any area that is marked with Xs is the place where you will possibly need this lightener.

We apply cover up lightener cream over the foundation rather than under foundation for two reasons.

1. It stays where it is put. Using it under the foundation is not as effective.
2. We want to have some of the lightness remain on the areas applied to give a brightness to that area.

In color theory, anything light or bright comes out to the eye; anything dark receeds back.

Cover up cream is a whitening agent that will hide circles under the eyes, etc. Most people use this only under the eyes.

18

SEASONS LIGHT AND COLOR GLOW
Face Conturing

CODE XXXXXXXXX **Lightener**
      XXXXXXXXX
      :::::::::: **Blusher**

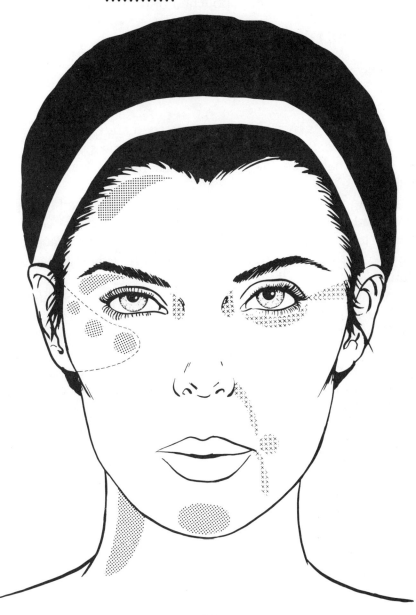

19

More can be done with it to soften your face lines and change the shape of your face.

In looking at your face straight-on in the mirror, examine the under-eye area. Do you have dark circles under the eyes? Are the circles under the eyes more pouched or what we call baggy?

DARK CIRCLES

Apply cover creme on all the very dark areas under the eye.

BAGGY EYES

Apply cover creme under the pouched area in just the dark lines. If you put the whitener on top of the puffiness you will bring out the problem area. Placing the white in the dark line under will help reduce the puffiness.

Using your moistened sponge that you have used to apply the foundation, pitty-pat over the whitener cover-up. This will blend it to your color but make the area still lighter. Wherever you use a cover-up cream, be sure to pat later with a little of the foundation to blend it in.

Our next area is the width of the temple or forehead right at the side of the eyes. If your area here is narrow, carry out the whitener from the corner of the eye to the temple. (as shown in the diagram)

Do not put white in this area if you have a broad area on each side of your eyes. This requires another treatment of contouring down the face.

Do you have any deep lines running down from the sides of the nose to the mouth? Or from the corner of the lips down to the chin? If so, work some of the whitener into the lines or crease area. Be sure to pat afterwards with the sponge and foundation.

If you have a deep chin line, soften here also with white.

Examine the face carefully for any shadow areas that detract from the softness of your complexion. Use the cover up cream in any shadow you want to hide.

For a narrow chin, apply white on both sides of the chin to broaden the look.

20

A little bit of whitener placed at the corner of the mouth on either side will lift the corners of the mouth.

READY FOR COLOR GLOW

Study your face carefully in a mirror. Notice the shape of your face. How closely does it fit into the perfect oval? Is it round, square, diamond, or perhaps heart shaped?

The face diagram is a perfect oval. One way to discover if you have areas that fall outside of an oval is to take a ruler and hold it lengthwise alongside the side of your eye, draw an imaginary line down your face from the top of the forehead to the chin area. Anything that falls outside of this area could be contoured down with color.

Is your forhead very short? Or is it very long?

Is your chin stubby or pointed?

We can do something about this with color. In contouring with color we use the blusher, either dry or cream, that matches your Season and apply in the following ways.

Blush should be applied first in three dots. One immediately under the colored portion of your eye, the next nearer the outer corner of the eye and the last farther out onto the temple area.

If your forehead is narrow, carry the blusher straight out to the temple, high up on the cheekbone. Do not go up to frame the eye.

For prominent cheekbones, stay right along the bone area and feather down a little in a shape similar to that shown on the chart.

For a wide forehead, carry blusher up onto temple area near the hairline without coloring the hair. This frames the eye with color and contours the face.

For high forehead, blend a little blusher at the top of the forehead near the hairline being careful not to mess up the hair with color.

For low forehead, whitener could be applied near the top of forehead.

Most everyone is terribly confused how to apply blusher on

21

the cheek area for face shape. If you will pull up the corner of your mouth and make an apple of your cheek, then you will find how to apply blush. Just follow the fattest area of the cheek.

One no-no . . . Do not apply any color any closer into the nose than the colored portion of the eye when looking out. To put color so close to the nose area squeezes in the look of your face.

Follow the basic diagrams for ways to use the blusher for your face shape. Some will tell you to use a wide white strip over the top of the cheekbone and just fill in the hollow with color. This does nothing to pick up the color of your eye.

In working with the *"Season's Lights and Color Glow"*© concept, we enhance the eye coloring and the Season's complexion coloring with correctly color-coded cosmetics. Every color we place on the face is correct for your Season.

When you follow this method of contouring with just lightener and blush for your Season, you will find that your Season's coloring is enhanced and you will be fashionably beautiful because your colors are right.

Blusher should be applied in other areas (see diagrams). Over the eyelids for the kiss of the sun effect, which also contours by making the upper eye area recede. This accents the eyelids.

Tip of the chin, to shorten or enhance the color. Springs can especially use a lot of color over the entire face.

Some may be applied to the tip of the nose area.

A trick to tie in your neck with the color of your face. Lightly apply blusher on the neck which lies under the blush area or cheeks, down to your collar (see diagram). This brings the eye up onto the face and puts you all together. Be sure to apply moisturizer to the throat area before doing this. Do not use foundation on the throat. It brings out lines and soils clothing.

CONTOURING THE EYES

If you can do your eyes in an attractive way, people will always notice you and think of you as beautiful. Not only do eyes tell us a lot about ourselves, they are expressive and should be enhanced with the right colors to bring out their beauty.

22

Most people do not have perfect shaped eyes. Either their lids are too large or small, or the eyes are deep-set or not deep-set enough. They may be too wide (away from the nose) or too close to the nose. The upper eye area above the lid and directly under the eyebrow may be too short or too straight or too puffy. This area may droop down, hiding the eyelids.

You may have gorgeous eyelashes, but most of us need to use color on them to thicken and make them longer.

The following diagrams and explanations should be of help to you in deciding how to make up your eyes.

The Normal Eye.

Eyes are considered normal if they are in correct porportion to the nose and face. The general rule of thumb is one eye length between the two eyes is normal as far as wide-set or close-set.

The eyebrows are arched perfectly and the space above the lid is about two times the height of the lid. The lid area is one-third of the space from upper lashes to the brow. The eye is open to show most of the iris. The eyelid itself is gently rounded and does not bulge or seem flat.

This is a wonderful area to show off color and like the perfect oval face, we can do just about anything we want with the normal eye.

GENERAL RULES OF THUMB IN MAKING UP EYES

As a student of Art, I was taught to fill up the canvas with paint. No area on the picture was left raw or unpainted. This is what we need to do with cosmetics on the face. Even if we add no color, we still need to cover the entire area. Foundation has been applied on the face and it should have been placed over the lid and under the eye also. If foundation and moisturizer has not been used, then eye makeup will not move easily for you.

When working with the eye area we need to work in patting, not pulling movements. The area of skin around the eye is different and more delicate than other areas of the face. It has no pores to become clogged. That is why we really see no blemishes surrounding the eye.

Those who wear contact lenses should be careful not to pull down the skin under the eye to the extent that the skin is stretched to cause wrinkles.

If you have allergies, try to get them under control because constant rubbing of the eye can pull and damage eye tissues.

Apply an eye cream for delicate tissues every night around the eye and on the lips. Sticks of Vitamin E oils are good for this also. Not only will they soften the lips and lubricate the eye tissue, it will also promote the growth of your eyelashes. Be sure to rub the cream or stick onto the lashes. This will also help if you have granulated eyelids or irritated eyes.

CONTOURING THE EYES WITH COLOR

We want to work with dark and toned down colors to recede eye areas. For areas we want to stand out or make larger, we will use lighter or brighter colors.

EYE COLORS

Several products will work for contouring.

1. Pencils for lining the socket of the eye and the crease of the eye, and for coloring the lid in some cases. The following pencils are appropriate for the Seasons.

Pearlized Highlighter, goes under eyebrow and a bit above the colored portion of the eye, on the lid to give is sparkle.

Black for a Winter

Light Purple - Compatible to all Seasons

Teal Blue   Autumn, Spring

Warm Brown   Springs and Autumns.

Light Blue   Summer or Winter.

Dark Blue   Winter.

Red Brown (wine color)   Sunset Winters

Green   Spring and Autumn

Grey   Summer and Winter

Medium Purple   Winter and Autumn

Coral   Spring and Autumn

2. Pressed Powder

Colors to bring out areas:

Summer — Blue, Pink

Winter — Light Plum, Light Blue, Silver

Spring — Aqua, Green, Peach

Autumn — Green, Bright Green

Colors to recede or lessen area of the eye:

Summer — Brown

Winter — Gray, Blue

Spring — Most Spring colors lighten.
         Use Tan or Greyed Tan.

Autumn — Olive Green, Brown.

Super Pearl shadows or Shimmer Dusts that will lighten and enlarge an area:

Summer — Light Blue, Silver, Rose.

Winter — Rose, Blue.

Spring — Green, Aqua, Yellowed Pinks.

Autumn — Green, Copper, Gold.

Winter — Plum, Brown, Red Gold

Spring — Brown

Autumn — Rust, Green Gold

ANY BRIGHTER COLORS CAN BE USED TO RECEDE AN AREA IF YOU WILL BRUSH GRAY OR BROWN PRESSED POWDER OVER TO DARKEN.

CANDLE GLOW — ANOTHER HIGHLIGHTER

Candle Glow may be applied directly under the brow from the center out, staying close to the brow. Also brush along the top cheekbone to enhance the cheekbone area.

EYES WITH A CHALLENGE

Lids That Hide Under Upper Eye Area

For your Season use an appropriate color from the bright and light eye products to apply directly on the eyelid. Make it even brighter by penciling with bright Highlighter Pencil over the color. Bring some of the lid color up onto the drooping lid on the outer area to make lids look larger. Draw in a fake eye crease with a Pencil or product for that purpose. Feather the color upwards to the brow. Keep highlighting pencil, shimmers, or Candle Glow high up under the brow. If eyes are small, just line with pencil and smudge the outer corner of the eye under the lashes. If eyes are normal size, line the dewey skin above the lashes with your Season's color. Use lots of Navy, Charcoal, Green, Black or Brown Mascara.

Puffy Upper Area

In this eye the upper area predominates and looks puffy. Use a receding color for your Season in a pencil, shimmer or pressed powder. Brush on the entire upper area to darken and make it recede. A neutral color is usually better here.

Bulging or Protruding eyes

With your Season's pencil in a darker color, line the entire dewey skin around the eye. then go over the top of the lashes with the pencil and lightly smudge. Always carry the color outside the outer corner of the eyes unless your eyes are extremely wide set.

Using a receding color, cover the entire lid to make it pull back. The lid will look dull and you will need to take some highlighting, lighter color or pencil, and highlight the inner corner if eyes are a bit close set to nose. Highlight the outer side if wide set away from nose. Do not put your highlighter in the middle. This will make the eye come forward again. Use some of the same lid color above the crease of the eye and use highlighter under the brow, lots of it, to take away from the bulge of the eye. Use a lot of mascara, brown or black.

Short Area Between Brow and Eyelid

You must be careful in this case to avoid darkening or putting too much color above the eye crease. Highlighter should be kept very narrow. If possible tweeze a lot of the underneath brows to give you more area to work with. If using *Brush On Brow*, always go above the brow first. Any heavier coloring should go above the brow.

Small Eyes

Using your pencil liner for your Season, line just the corner of the eye and extend the lining outward. Go above the lashes with a line of color and draw in a fake corner of the outer eye and smudge upwards. Choose a bright or enlarging color and apply shadow on lids working outwards and upwards up over the outer crease of the eye. This will make your eyes look much larger and open. Use a lot of mascara, concentrating on making the lashes on the top lid in the middle extra long.

Deep-Set Eyes

There is usually a very dark appearance in the eye-socket

which makes the eye seem deep into the area. The trick is to get enough light in this area to bring it out and keep the lid bright enough to show it up. Use cover up cream above the entire eye where there may be darkness. On the upper eye area, blend a slightly darker color to pull back the prominent bone. Use a bright color on the eyelid nearer the lashes and brighten with a highlighting pencil. Use the highlighter right under the brow area. In the crease of the eye use a light and bright product to bring out the crease if cover up cream has not lightened enough. If the eye still recedes back, brush on a shimmer or pearlized shadow to pull out the look.

Close-Set Eyes

To break the effect of the eyes being too close to the nose we want to do all of the eyelining, etc., about one-third away from the tear duct. In other words, do not put any color close to the inner corner of the eye to widen them. If eyebrows are close-set also, tweeze a little from the inner corners. With *Brush on Brow* in your color (Black, Charcoal, Dark Brown, Light Brown, Auburn or Blonde) brush on the color about the same area where eye color has been started and extend the brows out a little to widen the look there too.

Wide-Set Eyes

The complete opposite holds true with wide-set eyes. Line the eyes starting directly in the inner corner of the eye. Carry the lining out to about one-third away from the outer corner of the eye. Start lid color and upper eye area color right up to the inner side of the nose. Feather these out when you get to about one-third from the outer area of the eye. Fill in eyebrows a bit with *Brush On Brow* to make them just a little closer together over the bridge of the nose.

Oriental Eyes

This beautiful shape of eyes present a challenge because generally we have to decide what to do with them. I have found it better to accent the almond shaped eye rather than change it to something else. We generally find that the upper eye area is straight down to the eye opening and there is hardly any lid showing at all. Eye lining with pencils inside the dewey portion of the eyelid is impractical because it closes the eyes even more. Line the bottom of the eyelid under the lashes about half way out to the corner of the eye. Smudge slightly to soften. With a pretty colored eye pencil, or with the applicator filled with a receding color for your Season, draw in a fake eye socket area. About half way up between eyebrow and upper eye opening. Start directly in the inside corner of the eye and draw, arching upward near the middle and down again to the outer corner but not quite to the end (A moon shape arch). Smudge this up and fill the entire area with the darker color. Go close to the nose bridge and fill in all the way up to the eyebrow.

Lift the skin up that is lying over the eyelid and using a very bright, lightening shadow, cover the entire lid. Let the skin down and brush on the eye shadow or duster from about half way to the middle of the eye outward, winging up to the fake eye socket. This will enlarge the eyelid to some extent but still keep the lovely slanted, almond look that is so pretty.

30

MASCARA

At all times you should use the mascara most suited for your coloring. I usually choose black because it accents the eyes so beautifully. Mascara is better and less harsh if it does not contain fiber builders. It will build the lashes if you apply it, rolling the applicator brush as you go. It will help curl the lashes and put more color on them by applying them in this manner. If more color is desired, wait a few minutes, allow to dry, and apply again.

Brown is desirable on very fair people who have very light eyebrows. Mascara can be removed with some cleansers or special Mascara remover.

CONTOURING EYEBROWS

After the age of thirty, the skin on the face begins to stretch and give a little. This seems to be nature's way of giving us character as we age. When the skin on the forehead loosens, it lets the brows drop down. Have you ever noticed some older women who have a scowling appearance? If you consciously sit in front of

the mirror and let all the muscles relax, you might see what I am talking about. Once you are aware of how your face droops when you let it go, you will work harder at keeping the muscles toned up in the face and work at holding the skin muscles taut. We actually can have a younger appearance by lifting the forehead muscles and bringing up the corners of the mouth in a pleasant half smile. When we let the face droop we look much older.

To contour the brows, tweeze every bit you can from under the brow line, keeping your own natural arch. With *Brush On Brow* go into and above the brow with the color most like your hair coloring. Don't darken the brows a lot, just add shape.

Everyone has a bone that goes over the eye socket. This is your base for a brow. Feel this area. There is a bone directly above your socket. Now feel the eyebrow area. The top of the socket bone usually forms the shape of your brow.

Do not tweeze your brows out and draw fake lines. Keep your natural line if possible but work over it rather than in or under.

In order to do this, you must work the color slightly into the brow but the majority of the color line will fall just above the top of the brow.

Sometimes all the color that is needed is just a little touch at the end of the brow to lengthen it.

No matter what your Season is, choose the color according to hair shade, or better yet, to the natural coloring of the brow itself. You have been properly color-coded for your own unique personality and color scheme. It is always best to enhance rather than change those natural colors.

RESHAPING LIPS

The pencils we use for lining lips for the Seasons are

Winter — Plum or Red

Summer — Light Mauve or Pink

Spring — Coral Red or Yellow Brown

Autumn — Brown or Red-Orange

There are a lot of different products that may be used for coloring the lips. We always have to consider age, the degree of conservatism, and most importantly, your Season. Season dictates how much color and to what degree it should be used.

Do you remember when I told you a picture needs to be completely done with color or it will appear unfinished? To complete our face contouring and coloring we must put a finishing touch to your lips. This last little touch will add the parsley to a delightful dish.

Each person is completely individual when it comes to lipstick choice. Young girls prefer the feel of a lip glosser. Lipstick applied with the *Vitamin E Stick* under or over gives a creamy feeling to the lips also.

There are some who have come up through an era of naturalism and like completely bare lips. If I can persuade them to color I do. If not, I have to settle for the *Vita E Stick* or at least the *Lip Glossers* for each Season. (These are named for each Season with the addition of one called Spring-Autumn.)

A beautiful look is to line with the *Season's Pencil* and then use *Glosser* or *Vita E* on the entire lips for a very natural but finished appearance.

WHO NEEDS TO LINE THE LIPS?

I don't always line the lips with a lining pencil. I do if . . .

Lipstick tends to bleed.
Lips are too small or too large.
Lips are crooked and need line correction.

For those whose lipstick will not stay just on the lips but tends to bleed onto the outer area . . . The lips should first be powdered with a transluscent powder. Using either the lip lining pencil or a lipstick brush which has picked up some of the lipstick off your tube of lipstick; make a small cupie bow (see illustration) on the

top lip and follow the natural contour of the lips. Line into the corner only if your lips tend to droop. Now do the bottom lip.

For Large Lips

Line inside the natural lip line.

For Small Lips

Line on the outside of the natural lip line.

(Don't fool yourself into thinking you can hide a lot of the lip area with foundation or cover-up. Eventually your lips will peek out and all will see your lined area in an unnatural place.)

Now fill in the rest of your lips with lipstick color, *Glosser* or *Vita E Stick.* I hope to persuade you to use some lipstick color or gloss that I have coded to match your Season, because they will give you the color lift that you need. To concede to those conservatives who don't want much color, I will list our colors in two categories.

Conservative (lighter colors) Full Color (Intense, but right for your Season, too)

Summer —

Blue-Red	Pearlized Pink
Light Pink	Rose Gold
Brown Mauve	Light Raspberry

Winter —

Light Blued Coral	Plum
Frosted Red Violet	Dark Plum
Red Brown	Dark Raspberry

Spring —

Light Brown	Orange Coral
Brown Mauve	Bright Coral

Bright Red	Yellowed Pink
Corals	Yellow Tan

Autumn —

Frosted Brown	Red-Orange
Orange Brown	Bronze
Warm Brown	Copper

NAIL POLISH

It might seem strange to mention nailpolish here but most of the lipsticks have a matching or complimentary polish. Coloring the nails and how to do your own manicure will be taken up in another booklet. But think of how much your fingers are seen in

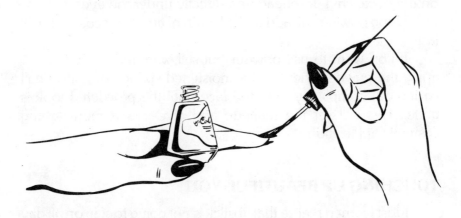

connection with your face. In talking and gesturing, as most of us do, the hearer not only hears what you are saying, he/she also sees your face and lips talking, plus your hands moving. How beautiful it is to see a correlation of hand color to face. Even if you have only used a glosser to give a finished look to the nails it will be more pleasing than just plain nails.

Being completely color correct from head to toe is so beautiful that even the most plain, the most ordinary person will seem extremely attractive.

SOME FINISHING TOUCHES

Who should powder? Face powder is not usually required but I find that a lot of Summer persons are more comfortable in a mat finish. Older women who are used to the mat look will like powder but sometimes they should not use it because the drier the face looks the more lined it will appear.

Those with oily complexions might need powder and even the dry blusher instead of cream. In using face powder use the *translucent loose* or *compact powder*. One shade will work for most persons.

The hairs on the face are called Cilia. They are so small we cannot see them with the naked eye but all of us have these little hairs growing on the face. when using face powder, work your puff in downward motions. This seals the makeup on the face. Applying a very fine film of powder is sometimes all that is needed on the nose, chin, forehead and directly under the eyes.

Using powder will add to the length of time your cosmetic will last.

If you want to use powder but still want that glow too . . . apply the powder, then with a moistened sponge or cotton ball wrung out completely, dab the face until the powdered look is gone. This will set the makeup and give you a more lasting cosmetic application.

TOUCHING UP BEAUTIFUL YOU

Most women realize that lipstick is not going to stay on all day and that they will need a little touch up at least after meals or before that man in your life comes home or you come home to him.

There isn't a cosmetic in the world that is so great that you will be completely perfect at the end of a day.

This is how I touch up for those special times and people in my life. When the glow is starting to fade I:

1. Apply just a bit more of *Cover Up Cream* under the eyes. (Remember now, this is a touch up, not a complete cleansing and

36

redo. If I am really going out for the evening to a very important affair or before a lecture, I start from the beginning for a complete overhaul and if I have time I lie down with *Spearmint Masque* on to rejuvinate the tired look at the end of the day.)

2. With a damp sponge I apply foundation over the cover-up under eyes, go over nose and chin.
3. Apply a little more blusher.
4. Just a tinge more eyeshadow on my lids. I use the high-lighting pencil under brow and above the eye.
5. More lipstick.

Wala! I am a new person and ready for anything.

Lipstick should be applied during the day whenever needed. If you are one of those pesons who expect a lipstick to stay on all day, you may want one that has an indelible quality. They are usually very dry but will last longer.

I would rather have a creamier feeling to the lipstick and apply it a time or two more during the day.

CANDLE GLOW

This is a pearlized finishing product that may be applied on cheekbones and upper eye areas under the brow or wherever you want a pretty pearlized glow.

I generally do not use *Candle Glow* for heavy faces. Like light, a shine will bring things out. Cheek bones are really pretty with a streak of light over them. In using a pearlizer be careful to avoid dulling the blush with it. If you know you are going to use this product, use more blush in the beginning.

SHIMMERY TOUCHES

Some of the brighter *Shimmery Eyedusts* are attractive when touched on the cheek areas and even in the hair or on the shoulders.

Cosmetics applied with the method of *"Seasons Lights and Color Glow"* are very refined and beautiful. The cosmetics are applied using a lot of color but there is a sheerness to the product *that lets your Season shine through.*

When you know your Season and use your proper clothing colors you enhance that beauty God gave to you. A beautifully applied, color coded cosmetic for your own personal color design will help you glow with color from head to toe.

FASHION LINE AND DESIGN
FOR YOUR SEASON
A Look at Your Individual Style

All of us want to look our very best in the clothing we can afford. It is not vanity, but an inner pride that tells us we want to be respected by others. Most of us never have enough clothing to suit all of our needs. If we do, sometimes we choose unwisely and we find ourselves in a predicament of not having the proper piece of clothing for a special occasion.

In my book, **"Color Me A Season"** How to Find and Use Your Most Flattering Colors, there are some beginning helps in starting a wardrobe with the proper colors for yourself. This booklet will, I hope, help you to achieve your proper Season's appearance, but go into a more individualistic approach as you choose your clothing for your own distinct personality.

Several aspects enter into the purchasing of clothing for ourselves.
1. Lifestyle — the need for specific items of clothing
2. Age and personality type
3. Economic situation
4. Figure type
5. Your Season (personal color design)

LIFESTYLE

You and I probably have an entirely different need for clothing. As a color analyst and lecturer, I need clothing that will see me through appearances and engagements. My first consideration is to be an example of what I teach in color. There are no days of sloughing off for me in wrong colors. If I go downtown in a "Spring" colored blouse (myself a Winter) I am sure to see ladies whom I have color-coded or who have seen me lecture about color, and so you see, I have a specific need to be dressed properly in color. My profession calls for more clothing than the norm. My needs then are different from yours.

39

What is your lifestyle? Are you a homemaker? Do you work? Where?

The working woman's wardrobe will be much different from the homemaker. She needs to coordinate her apparel and carefully add to her wardrobe to be presentable to the public.

If you work in an office that has very few people coming and going, you can get by with fewer clothing items.

When working where you see the same individuals who are important to the business, at least once a week, you need to consider trying to have enough clothing changes to be coordinated differently every day, but in as few items as possible.

When you know your Season, you can take advantage of your color bouquet of at least sixteen or more base colors. How you use those colors depends a great deal upon your own personality and lifestyle.

The homemaker has a little more freedom to choose her clothing for comfort and for color that might not otherwise be done in a busy office. For instance, a Spring person might very much enjoy her Spring red in a suit for the office but her job might call for more conservative color. If so, she might choose a pretty yellow gray suit and use the bright red for her blouse. She will be in correct color all over her body, but in a more conservative way. Our homemaker could choose a colorful red print housedress, brightening up herself and her home and still be properly dressed for her situation and her Season.

Lifestyle includes our social life, too. One who has a lot of party occasions will of course need more than one party dress for her social whirl. She might need to put some thought into coordinating a party wardrobe of skirts, blouses, pretty shawls and jackets that will make a few things look like different outfits.

Jot down on a piece of paper all the places you go where you wear clothing; home, work, taking the children to lessons, little league ball games, parties, etc. Put them all down. Now underline the ones that need a definite change of clothing from what you would ordinarily wear at home all day. Take a critical look at the list and try to determine how you could dress up or down one basic piece of clothing so it would fit all occasions. Let's see . . .

40

8:00 A.M. dressed for the day in a blue skirt and white cotton blouse, comfortable tennis shoes for working around the house (consider a good arch supporting shoe instead). 11:45 to the school to pick up the children; slip on your sweater or jacket. Going in to talk to the teacher? Change shoes to casual but dressy shoes. Home again for lunch and more work; back to the tennies again. Club meeting at 3:30; slip into a casual but pretty print overblouse and pull the white collar over the neck opening. Belt it with a matching color to your casual dressy pumps; purse and coat and you are ready to go. Home again to freshen up for your date with hubby at the bowling alley. Change into blue slacks and tennies; off and running, and that's how it goes.

Exaggerated as this is, there are some times that we are so busy we are on the run without much chance for careful clothing changes.

Your lifestyle is really so different from anyone elses that it is difficult to put down clothing choices without really doing a personal analysis of your wardrobe. You will have to do that yourself from the things we discuss in this booklet.

AGE

Of course it is important to consider how young or old you are when deciding what is proper for your wardrobe. I personally feel most people should dress fairly much for their Season, rather than costuming themselves in *little girl* or *old lady* dresses. You have a feeling about that within yourself; something that says, "I'm not comfortable in that," or "I feel just great wearing this outfit."

Be sure you are wearing clothing that is right for you and not your daughter. There are a few older women who have such darling figures they have a tendency to get into the teenage closet and wear and borrow clothing items. It's usually an entirely different look and not sophisticated enough for them. Age brings with it a touch of conservatism, even for Springs.

A Spring person who is no longer in the teen category, can get that bright feeling in her colors rather than in the teen styles of a

41

younger girl.

A younger Winter girl might have a tendency to dress too elegantly for her age. She needs the addition of time to become a classic Winter. Meantime, by staying within her color range and keeping her wardrobe simple, she will achieve the correct fashion look for her age and for her Season.

There seems to be a division of four periods of our lives that affect our clothing choices.

1. Childhood
2. Teen years
3. Adult
4. Senior Adult

Here again, many people have a feeling where they belong. They want to fit in with their peers. Lifestyle again enters in. Where we go and what we do dictates the type of clothing that we wear.

I am a strong believer in letting people choose what they want to wear. I am not a terribly fashion conscious person, in that I hope my image is not that of *high* fashion. I admire and appreciate those who can be fashionably correct all the time, but I have too much to do in my life to be overly conscious of every new style that comes out. My writing and cosmetic business plus color analysis keeps me so busy that I hardly have time for shopping around.

I have come to realize, however, that it makes life a lot more simple to study clothing choices and coordinate your wardrobe. I try now to follow some of the advice of experts in the field and find that I usually have something to wear if an occasion arises without rushing down to the department store to get a new dress.

I recently purchased, on an impulse, a fake fur cape. I love it and it looks terrific on me. It's my color, my style, but the problem is I haven't had one occasion yet to wear it. I have put it on several times but it is too dressy for any occasion that has come up yet. As it looks now, I will get to wear it about ten months from now at my husband's office Christmas party, which is the most formal occasion I go to.

That kind of purchasing is unfortunate and what I hope to eliminate for me and for you in future shopping sprees.

Our Season affects our clothing purchases. I, as a Winter,

simply love the dressy, the elegant, the rich things hanging on the racks out there. Though I like dressing up like a princess there isn't much occasion to wear that type of clothing for me at the present time.

Your Season does the same thing to you. If you are Summer, you probably are super conservative with clothing, especially color. Summers do not make enough of a clothing statement in the things they wear.

Springs have to guard against purchasing clothing that catches their eye. They like color, but tend to have too many casual things and not enough for dress-up.

Autumns probably do the best in purchasing their clothing. Their style is practical, smart and sophisticated. If anything, their wardrobe might be a little sparce for dress-up occasions.

ECONOMIC SITUATION

If you don't have money, you can't buy it. That used to be a hard and fast rule of economics. We really need to budget carefully for clothing and avoid abusing credit cards.

I have a really fun time bargain hunting. We have in the San Francisco Bay Area, several wholesale factory outlet places that are just delightful to browse through.

A smart shopper will ferret out those places in her community that offer real bargains. One or two purchases can soon tell you if a place is offering lower priced goods or if they are actually giving the customer a good deal on some of the name-brand clothing.

Have you ever purchased a dress or blouse that in a few wearings and washings turns out to be an ugly dud? I have. That's where experience pays off. Look at seams and the way buttons are sewn on. Check labels for fabric content and washing instructions.

I recently purchased a blouse that goes so well with a particular suit that I got it even though I knew it was part acetate. I knew it would present washing problems. I have to iron it, which I simply detest to do. It is showing wear already, but I like the appearance of it so much I am babying it along for as many

43

wearings as I can get out of it. The only time that I will ever purchase something that requires that much care is if it is so attractive I can't replace it with a better quality item. Thank goodness the blouse was on the bargain rack so I won't lose much when it gives out.

I allow more in my clothing budget now than I did in the days that my five children were home and in need of clothing too. I did a lot of home sewing for myself then and none at all now, because of my schedule, but I really like to bargain hunt. Let's talk a little about that.

IS IT OR ISN'T IT A BARGAIN?

I don't think I will ever forget reading an Ann Landers column about a frustrated wife who wrote in about her husband buying fifteen brooms because they were bargains. If you already have ten blouses in your closet, you don't need another one. A bargain is only a bargain if you need it. Just because it is cheaper you may be better off saving that money and putting it towards a more basic suit or coat.

Some bargains are leaders that are brought into chain stores, in particular, for special sale. They are designed to get you in the store. The clothing is sometimes good quality but going out of style.

Has this ever happened to you? Just when you can finally afford a new style that you have been dying to wear, it suddenly is dated before you have worn it very long? The reason for the bargain is that the store knows it is either a dead item or will soon be unfashionable.

Clothing is sometimes put on the bargain rack if it is a bad fit. I ran into a terrific sale of slacks. The material was excellent and the price was great, but I soon found what the problem was. The legs of the pants were unusually full. They were sloppy and obviously a pattern error. When you find a rack of many of the same kind of garments, you might be encountering something like this. There is some reason these particular clothing items have not sold. Check them out carefully and be sure to try them on with a critical eye.

44

Material types and colors that have been fashionable are often finally put on the bargain tables to clear them out because something new is coming in. Right now the new velours in brilliant colors are all the rage. You see the material featured in bright colors in blouses and one-piece dresses. At first they appeared a few at a time in more expensive clothing stores. We all wanted these and so they are now featured in some of the less expensive chain stores.

A dress or blouse like this is fun to have if you only get one. Be sure not to waste your clothing budget on too many fad items because the look will soon be out of style and you will feel self-conscious wearing an obviously dated dress.

An exception might be made here if your Season happens to be Winter and you get it in just the right color. You will be able to use it longer because it is your style and fashion look, particularly if it has a sheen to it. A Winter could get by with a black velour dress for some time and might even add a layered look to it with an underblouse or an overjacket.

It took me years to catch on to this little trick of the fashion trade. After everyone has purchased the new fashion, they change to get you to buy again. There are always, however, the tried and true fashions that are there if you know where to look for them.

There are two particular stores that I shop in that have racks for discount sales. They are there all the time and they put items on sale which for some reason or other have not sold. Every time I go into those stores for any reason, I check out these racks. A jacket that had been selling for twenty-five dollars finally wound up on the rack for five. It was a terrific color for me. It's problem was that the matching skirt which was twenty dollars was no longer with it and I guess the store felt no one would want it alone. I did, and it has served me well. It is a light Winter plum color which I wear over darker plum pants and skirt.

You may find a belt missing on a particular item that you could replace with something at home. Sometimes a hem is out or a tiny seam rip makes it unsaleable at the regular price. Rather than take a complete loss on these items, the stores get what they can (usually their cost or less).

One of my husbands aunts had superb taste in clothing. I loved to see her in her pretty clothes. She never spent a great deal on anything but watched carefully at her favorite stores for sales and bargains. Often times she would find a dress she really wanted for full price, but would patiently wait until the sale days and then hurry down to be there first in line to (hopefully) find her desired object of apparel hanging on the rack marked down to a more affordable price. If it was still too high to fit her clothing budget, she would take a chance and let it hang a few more days until the final markdown. If she got it, she was elated; if not, she realized she couldn't have afforded it at a higher price and set her sights on another dress. Her wardrobe was well thought out and each purchase was planned for.

RUMMAGE OR TREASURE

You would be surprised at what some people throw away. If you have the time to scout around at rummage sales and flea markets, you can come up with some unusual items to add to your wardrobe at fantastic prices.

Usually the clothing you find will be outdated and worn. There is always a chance that someone might have gone into a larger size and has let go of a fairly good item of clothing. It should be checked carefully, of course, to see if it is stained or soiled under the arms. It should be gone over for rips or tears or any such thing to discover why it is being sold.

One has to be very careful about clothing purchases, but . . . some fun things to find at such sales are:

Jewelry and accessories; reusable trims and buttons on some worn-out clothing. Without realizing the value, people tire of jewelry and many times you will find some interesting pieces. For instance, I have some gold colored pieces that do not fit my Season. I never wear them and they are too mature for my Spring daughters. These would most certainly be sale items if I could ever find time to have a garage sale.

One very fashionable person I know found an old coat

trimmed with fur. She didn't use the coat, but found a perfect trim for a beautiful suit she was making.

Very pretty and unusual buttons are sometimes found on out-of-fashion clothing. With the price of buttons now, it pays to purchase the garment and use them.

I used to feel guilty about destroying a garment in this way, but would try to use the material even for quilt blocks or as a good rag. Everything has to come to an end sometime when it's original use has been ended.

Very good zippers can be removed and saved for future home sewing. You have to figure the time cost to you. If you have time, it is worth it.

Some darling stuffed toys and doll clothes can be made from old clothing.

I know that some people cut all the buttons and zippers off a dress and then give it to the goodwill. To me this isn't sharing. If I have something good enough for someone else to wear, I would rather they get full use of the entire piece than just a cut up rag.

SHOPPING FOR THE BEST or
NOT NECESSARILY A BARGAIN

There are just some times when bargain clothing will not do. Special items should be chosen with great care and concern.

If one plans ahead far enough in advance, bargain sales can be taken advantage of.

If you know that your winter coat is wearing out, you would be wise to seek out those coat sales that happen at the end of the winter season when things are marked down almost fifty percent. The before-school sales in August and September also feature markdowns on the new coats. Some of these are probably ones that did not sell from last year's merchandise, but others are really the brand new fashions for the current year.

A coat, suit or very basic piece of clothing that is expected to last at least two or three years should not be sacrificed for on the bargain market. It is something you are going to have to live with for a long time and you want the very best style and line for you.

Purchasing a coat in an odd color or style because it is cheaper is not very wise. It will hang in your closet unused or make you very uncomfortable when you wear it.

Skirts will last longer than blouses and tops, and if you have chosen wisely, you will have a usable garment for many years; changing the look of it with different fashionable tops, blouses, sweaters and vests. It stands to reason that more money should be spent on that particular item in your wardrobe.

Slacks tend to wear out faster than skirts because they are worn for more casual wear. You can wear the crotch right out of a pair of pants if you wear them a lot. Knees tend to get a little stretched and frazzled looking, too. Since this is a changeable item anyway, a little less of our clothing budget might be spent on it. It is always nice though to have a really good dressy pair of slacks that will go with a favorite blazer and vest. A non-wearout material is a smart buy here.

Choose your basics with care and let the thrifty side come out when it comes to more changeable items. It is fun to have one or two fad dresses or blouses. A suit should never be chosen in a faddish style that can only be worn a short time because too much money is invested.

You are fortunate if you can do some of your own sewing to save a little money on your clothing allowance.

Sewing makes possible a nice wardrobe that otherwise could not be purchased.

When I see the price of materials today, I wonder just how much we save. I think we have to know the fabric store that has the best materials for the best buys and ones who really feature bargain material closeouts at certain times of the year.

One of the fabric stores in my area has leader items and whenever I have gone in to purchase material, I am disappointed because I have never found the really good materials on sale. Most of the sale items are in pieces of three to five yards pulled out of shape, ugly colors, etc. The rest of the materials are super expensive, so I hardly ever go there.

In comparison, there are other stores who really do offer good markdowns to close out their seasonal materials.

Colors sometimes become unfashionable because they have been overworked. I have been told that colors are chosen seven years in advance for the fashion market. This is because all buttons, thread, zippers, etc., must be created at the same time to go with the featured color for a certain year.

Have you ever purchased a piece of material and let it lie for a long period of time and then decide to make it into something? Were you able to match buttons and zippers with it? Sometimes it is hard to find the exact color you need, so I suggest if you store material, choose the buttons and sewing notions you need when you buy it. You can usually match up thread, but buttons can be a real problem.

If the color is unfashionable but it fits you and your Season, do not be afraid to get it, because people will love it on you anyway. I would steer away from a certain material type that might become dated rather than a color. As an example of this, polyester knit materials were so popular for awhile. Matching pantsuits were made of the solid color slacks and a corresponding print was used for the top in the same color polyester. This became Mrs. America's costume. The material was so comfortable, so washable, so wearable, everyone had at least one in their wardrobe. Usually a little matching scarf was worn at the neckline, and pretty loop earrings on your ears and you were set for an afternoon out with the girls.

All of a sudden it is no longer fashionable to wear one of these creations. Why? Because the creativity was taken out of our hands and the look became a uniform. The material was overdone. I think the fashion industry really had a hard time weaning us away from those double knits because they were easy to sew and would last forever.

I quit sewing when the polyesters were taken over by cottons again. I was spoiled by the ease of this fabulous material. Perhaps when our oil situation is resolved and other materials go out, we will get our double knits back again in something new and creative.

I love the blended fabrics that do not need ironing, and those that do not wrinkle. Wool is still the finest material to work with to make tailored items, but it is sometimes disappointing to me because even though it is beautiful when you press it, after first sitting it may become wrinkled.

If you choose a wool or any other material, grab the corner of the material and squeeze for all your might. If it wrinkles, you will have the same problem when you wear it.

Personally, I feel we live in a technical enough age that non-wrinkling materials should be produced for us. They in themselves are energy savers when we do not have to press them with irons, etc., and can use low heat to wash and dry. Watch out when you are bargain hunting for fabric. Make sure it will not shrink, wrinkle, bleed color, etc., before you buy it.

I purchased some cotton blend material to make a simple dress and was so disappointed in it. At first wearing I wound up with turquoise stains under my arms. This was a first rate fabric store and the material was overpriced for the quality. Live and learn.

Most fabric stores will stand back of their materials, so they should return your money for anything like this. Check the bolt for information and ask the sales clerk if the fabric is fade proof, etc. If a company will not offer a moneyback guarantee for their product, then you know they aren't sure of its quality either. There are other stores who will accept returns of bad merchandise.

If It's Washable, Preshrink

Be sure to wash any washable fabric and the notions that will be used in sewing it. Dry according to instructions BEFORE you make it into your garment. This will save you a lot of problems later and keep your completed outfit as perfect as it was before you washed it.

Follow the same instructions for store bought garments also. I found the most terrific pair of slacks that fit me perfectly, except they were too long. Generally you can get by with altering clothing that has been factory made before it is washed; not so with this pair. I now have one pair of slacks two inches too short. Be sure to pre-wash bluejeans, especially before hemming for length.

Choosing the Right Pattern

To me, choosing the pattern is the number one important

50

step in creating a piece of clothing suitable for our individualistic personality and figure type. We will go into details on figure types later. First, let's talk about patterns.

There are several types of patterns from different companies. A seamstress must realize that some are easier to follow than others. Simplicity and McCalls are the easiest for me. Butterick and Vogue are the choice my daughter Nora makes because she is a little more accomplished at the sewing machine. She has had specialized clothing classes and some tailoring instructions.

Follow the directions on the pattern like a roadmap. Beginners sometimes do a better job on their sewing because they are more careful about doing it right. Thirty-three years of sewing have given me license (I think) to ignore the directions. I have no desire to do tailoring and I want a quick and easy pattern.

In looking at the picture of the pattern, we have to realize that this is sometimes the artist's conception of the garment. The figure drawing is sometimes done out of proportion to make the design more attractive. You have to visualize yourself in that pattern. If the model's legs are very long and yours are short, imagine shorter legs. If you are large in the bosom and the model is very flat-chested, you have to think of the change that would make in the final picture.

They just never have bad figure faults in the pictures on the patterns. They want to sell them and all the garments will be especially appealing. It makes the choice difficult.

Usually they are pictured in a color that is compatible to the style. Sometimes the color is appealing to you, but you should visualize it in different colors. Ask yourself, "Is this pattern something a Summer, etc., could wear? If it were in a Summer color would it be attractive on me?"

Second big step — does the pattern go with the fabric you have chosen? How do you choose patterns? — After picking out the fabric do you choose the style first, and then the fabric?

Sometimes you just get inspired by a certain piece of material and like it so much you pick a pattern to fit it. Other times you have a certain style in mind. Choose it first, and then pick a material to fit it.

51

I think the second way is the best. This means that before you went to the fabric store, you had a particular piece of clothing in mind; something that you needed to add to your wardrobe.

Remember our fashion looks for the Seasons:

Summer — Romantic (softly feminine)

Spring — Natural (funwear)

Autumn — Sophisticated (businesslike)

Winter — Elegant (dramatic richness)

Whatever your Season is, you would do well to consider the pattern and the material to make sure you will be achieving the type of garment suitable to your personality.

EXPLORING THE YIN YANG THEORY

Some controversies have existed between those who teach the Yin Yang theory of body type and the Season's theory of clothing that each person should wear. I believe that these things can be cleared up by careful study of eye pattern and the realization that we are going to inherit different physical characteristics from our parents.

"Color Me A Season" contains general rules that apply for each season. We are all complete and different individuals and yet we fit into one of four color areas. We are individuals within our color area. My best color might be Winter's blue; another person's, Winter's yellow. What makes the difference? Physical characteristics, hair and eye coloring, and personality.

Let's explore the Yin and Yang of it. This theory dates back to the ancient Chinese who were aware of face types and body structure. They divide figure types into six areas.

1. Dramatic
2. Athletic
3. Classic
4. Romantic
5. Gamin
6. Ingenue

Picture the following types:

Dramatic

Above average in height, this figure type is large boned, long legged, erect posture. Head is oval with high cheekbones. Eyes are deepset, sometimes slanted or at an angle with heavy lids. Eyebrows are sharply defined. Nose is long, pointed, flared at the nostrils. Lips are held firmly and they are either thin or heavy. Body coloring is striking, contrasting. Personality is reserved, perhaps evey haughty.

Athletic

Also above average in height with a sturdy, stocky build, hands held on hips, square jaw. Average sized eyes with heavy dark eyebrows. Strong nose, large or irregular in some way, wide mouth. The Athletic has a free and open personality.

Classic

Average in height and well-proportioned, poised and well-balanced with an oval head. Eyes are average with eyebrows forming a pleasing arch. Nose and mouth are well shaped. The classic is gracious, well-mannered and mature.

Romantic

Average in height with a feminine well-rounded rigure, long legs. She stands gracefully. The face is heart or triangular and considered quite beautiful. Eyes, too, are large and alluring with arched eyebrows. Delicate nose, long, straight with a slight turn up. Full curved lips. The romantic is charming with a flirtatious feminine manner.

Gamin

Below average with small bones, she is well coordinated and stands with a perky hands-on-hips manner. Face is small, rounded with wide open, wide apart twinkling eyes. Eyebrows are natural. Nose is turned up, sometimes referred to as a button nose. Mouth is small and rounded. The Gamin has a tomboy, young expression.

Ingenue

Tiny and small boned with a delicate air. She is very appealing. Round cheeks and chin. Wide set eyes which are round and long lashed. Eyebrows form a delicate natural arch.

Dainty nose with a rosebud mouth. The Gamin is bubbly and demure.

Did you find yourself here? I would not be surprised if you found yourself in more than one body type. People do inherit different physical features from parents of different body types. We are all Heinz variety and yet we can combine the body pattern types with our coloring and come up with an attractive fashion look for ourselves.

The Winter person would best be described as a Dramatic because of the contrasting character of skin tone and coloring. Some Winters, however, are romantics or Classics, depending on body types.

Can you see where the difference lies between Seasons and Yin Yang?

In body analysis, the Summer personality might find herself in the Classic or Ingenue. Romantic would even be a possibility.

A Spring most definitely fits into the Gamin or Athletic area. If she has a parent, however, who is a Winter Dramatic, she might inherit the build of the Dramatic and the skin coloring of Spring.

An Autumn could be described as Athletic or Classic.

In studying our eye patterns, we can almost see two or three blends of personality. We should then realize that it is possible for our bodies to be blends of the Yin Yang theory.

Colors should be worn that are flattering to our skin tone. If our body structure does not quite fit into the Season's fashion look, then adjustments must surely be made. We do this by observing the entire figure and doing a personal analysis of its flaws and perfections.

I like the Season's theory of color and clothing because usually the skin tone of an individual will fit into the personality type enough that the kind of clothing, or at least the colors of the color bouquet, are flattering to the individual. Adjustments are made to suit the person without putting them into tight little compartments of either behavior or style.

We find all Yins and Yangs in all Seasons. Naturally, if you are a Summer person who is larger in stature, you will want to adjust the tiny laces and prints of Summer.

An especially large framed and tall Summer can still remain soft and delicate in a soft angora type sweater and larger plaid skirt in her colors rather than an overall tiny flower print dress. She can, if she likes, choose a more tailored suit in a soft gray brown or one of her neutral tones and make a blouse that has a delicate print in soft pastels. We have helped her keep her understated color look in something that blends with her dresden-like skin tone.

If perchance our Summer is overweight, we would not expect her to wear a light overall print design, though it sometimes might be refreshing for her to wear one. We would instead encourage her to, either by the line and cut of the pattern, or by using her darker colors, make a garment that would be more slimming to her as an individual.

Often the individual who has a few extra pounds will appear slimmer in her own colors because the eye is drawn to the face when properly color-coded.

There are darker colors in each Season's Bouquet that may be used to good advantage.

In the case above, it would be the same for all of the Seasons. They should adjust their style and color from their own Bouquet to help in their figure problems.

COLOR CAMOUFLAGE

From **"Color Me A Season"** I will repeat:

Color in our apparel can be useful to us as it is in our homes. Color can cause optical illusions and our figures will appear more perfect than they actually are. Knowing how to use color to correct problems in our lives can make us happier.

TWO RULES OF INTENSITY

1. Brightness and light stand out and make areas look larger.

2. Darkness and shade make areas recede and seem smaller.

RULES FOR USING COLOR

1. In fashion, never use more than three colors, two are better.
   a. A print with many colors is the exception. In that case, use only one other color for contrast.

2. When several colors are used in one composition, arrange them in pleasing proportions. Equal amounts will not be interesting.

3. Laws of areas — keep stronger colors (in hue, value, or intensity) in smaller areas. Use this color to attract attention to a desirable center of interest.

4. For harmony and unity of costume, repeat color in a smooth, not jerky way. This is called rhythm.

Let us deal with the LAW OF AREAS in color camouflage, attracting attention to a desirable center of interest.

What is the most pleasing, well-formed area of your figure? Use your stronger more intense color there to keep the eye in this area. Use duller, darker colors in the ill-proportioned areas to hide them.

The following diagrams illustrate figure faults and how to use color to correct them.

Average

The average figure can use color in any way that pleases the individual. Keep in mind bright colors make you look larger. If this is not a problem, wear them and enjoy them.

Inverted Triangle

This is the person with extra wide shoulders or a very large bust. More subdued colors should be used on the top. A dark jacket the same color as the skirt or pants would give the top a slimming effect. Skirts can be pleated or gathered. Color in pockets at hip area would widen the image. Bright colors may be worn below waist area.

Triangle

This is the big hips and legs figure. Keep bright colors and interest above the waist. Subdued or darker colors (for low-scale interest) should be worn below the waist. Use simple, straight, slightly flared skirts and pants or slacks with no interest stitching, pockets, etc., at the hipline.

Curvy

Bright or light areas of color running up and down with darker or more subdued colors on the outside of the figure area are suggested. For example, a dark navy dress with a white stripe running up and down either in the center or to one side.

Too Tall 5′9″

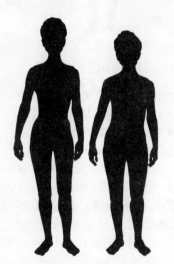

Wear separate colors, or all one color outfits broken by another color, such as a belt or a ruffle. Use inserts of contrasting colors. Color interest may be used in large purses, jewelry and accessories.

Too Thin

Use brighter, lighter colors in lines that are softly bloused or flared. Skirts gathered or pleated all around. Contrasting colored belts are helpful. Color interest in collars and bow ties, bracelets, multi-strand necklaces and scarves are flattering. Light colored stockings will make the legs appear to be larger.

Too Short Under 5′4″

Wear verticle lines not cut by a colored belt or trim. Wear one color outfits in perfect proportion to your petite size. Keep eye catching colors and details at neckline and shoulder area to draw interest to the upper part of the figure. Colored prints should be small, no large colored designs.

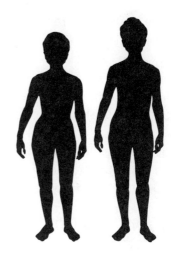

Protruding Tummy

Choose a one color outfit with a self-belt or none at all. Keep fullness at stomach area. Skirts with front gathers and jackets that cover are very concealing. Choose things that are slightly bloused above the waist. Use colored accents at shoulder area under contrasting color collars or interesting necklines. Draw attention away from it by using colorful scarves at the neck.

FACE SHAPE AND LENGTH OF NECK

The type of dress collar can be important to the facial shape.

ROUND FACES

Never accent a round face with a round collar. A Peter Pan type is especially bad. What you need is a V-necked blouse with a pointed collar opened up to about the second button. This will give you added length. It is also helpful to wear a long chain that comes down in a V shape, especially one that has a focal point hanging at the end. The weight of the stone or medallion, etc., keeps the chain in a V position which is slimming to the round face. If you have a large bosom, be sure the chain does not dangle over the bustline from a sideview position.

Square collars can also accent the roundness of your face. Sometimes if you wear a scoopneck dress, it will be attractive because the roundness of the neck opening is far enough away from the chin to give length to the face and neck.

SQUARE FACES

Do not wear a square collar with a square face. The same kind of neckline for round face is attractive on you. An oval neckline is nice and scallops (when in style) are too. In principle, we find that a rounded or oval neckline or rounded lines will cut the squareness of the square face.

ANGULAR FACES

This type of face shape needs rounded lines or oval necklines to break the angular face shape. Necklaces that form rounded lines rather than a V are better.

SHORT NECKS

An open V neck is nice for a short neck. The collar may stand up somewhat in the back of the neck as long as it is open in the front to elongate the neckline.

Cowl necklines or turtleneck sweaters are not very attractive on this type of neck.

When scarves tied around the neck are fashionable, twist yours until the part being placed around your neck is like a fine rope. Tie the scarf as low on the neckline as possible.

LONG NECKS

V necklines can accentuate the longness. Wear instead,

something that comes up onto the neck area such as a cowl neck sweater or dress. Turtleneck is great, also laces or collars that fit well above the shoulder line onto the back and front of the neck. Scarves, when in fashion, are very good for you since they break the long line of the neck. Fold the scarf and leave the portion that goes around your neck about two inches wide. Tie midway on the neck.

Jewelry should be worn high on the neck avoiding any long chains, etc. A filled-in look is good with lots of chains in your Season's metal color will fill in the space of a long neck.

Hairstyles are also important and can help a great deal in correcting the face shape or length of neck. This is covered in "A Crowning Glory for Your Season."

THE BLACK AND WHITE OF FASHION LINE

We have our figure charts showing how to wear color for camouflage. Let's consider now the actual line or cut of clothing and which are best for you.

VERTICAL LINES — We always think of one line up and down as being very slenderizing. We make a vertical line by the seams of clothing, the way the buttons are sewed on, or in trims going up and down. Who should wear the vertical line? Everyone except the very tall person or one who is very thin and willowy.

The vertical line is not always slimming. When many vertical lines are used together side by side (such as in a pleated skirt) the effect is broadening to the figure. Large or bright colored stripes can make you look heavier also.

HORIZONTAL LINES — The same line that goes up and down to slim can do a turnabout when it runs around the figure. It affects the figure differently in this case.

Place a horizontal seam or a line formed by the end of a long jacket low on the body and we get the effect of shortness. This of course is great for a very tall person.

A horizontal line formed by waist high jacket, belt or other line cutting the figure midway, shortens somewhat by cutting the figure in half, but it also can make the waist seem larger unless the belt or line is very narrow and in a self-covered fabric.

The shorter person who wants to appear taller can use the horizontal line to advantage by wearing it high on the body, such as under the bustline in an empire style dress. You will seem much taller. Here again a wide strip of color or stripes going across the bustline itself can make it seem fuller which may or may not be what is needed for your figure type.

SKIRT LINES

The way the material is sewn from the waist down can make a tremendous difference on you. Skirt styles which are considered fashion lines are:

The Sheath — a very slim, straight up and down skirt that adds height but is difficult to wear because you must have a perfect figure to wear it.

The A-Line — a gently flared skirt line that has more fullness over the hips and at the hemline than the sheath. It is much more flattering for all figure types because of the fullness to hide figure problems below the waist. It still gives a vertical look that will not cut your height.

The Flared — very full at the hemline and narrow at the waist. This skirt line tends to shorten a heavier or shorter person. It is very good for the tall or thin person.

The Pleated Skirt — this skirt can be very deceiving for figure types. Much depends on how the pleats are sewn in, what type of material is used, what print is chosen and the color. This is a garment that must be tried on to see its effect. Generally you will find that if you are hippy or heavy through the waist, this is not the skirt type for you.

Pleats are either sewn down about to the hipline or not sewn down at all. Sewn in pleats can seem like a girdle and it takes a super thin person to wear them.

Soft pleats are also hard to wear because if you have any tummy protruding, the pleats will stand out also.

The Gathered Skirt — the material may be slightly gathered

at the waist and flare out at the bottom. This is a becoming style for most everyone especially if it is sewn in a soft material.

A gathered skirt that we used to call a dirndle is as wide at the top as at the bottom and a gathering thread pulls the top into tiny gathers which are sewn onto a waistband. The very thin person can wear this well. One who has big hips and tiny waist can also use it to advantage. It has the tendency to shorten the figure.

If you have a protruding tummy or buttocks, don't try to camouflage them with this skirt. It makes you look like a potato sack pulled in at the middle.

FIGURE FLAWS

Full Bust. If you will keep the area from your shoulder to your waist as simple as possible you will draw less attention to the bust and more to your face. Always have your cosmetics on perfectly and draw attention to a lovely hairstyle or interesting scarves of jewelry (earrings are especially good).

Use dull finishes in the fabric for the top portion of the body in darker or more subdued colors. Stay within your Season for color but wear the lighter or brighter colors down in the skirt or slacks area. Example: A Winter could wear a black, simple blouse with a pair of white or gray slacks. Balance the color out with black shoes and brighten the face with lovely colors on your face; bright lipstick and pretty earings, etc.

Material types make a difference, too. Do not use transparent fabrics or ones that cling. Sweaters and knits are examples of this. Bodices should be loose, not tight. Use V or scoop necklines. No jewelry or flowers please, on the problem area. Balance out your look with a slightly flared skirt or one with pockets or other details. Fuller jackets and coats are better than fitted.

Narrow Shoulders. I have never thought of shoulders as a problem, but one day while shopping in a large mall, a woman approached me coming from the opposite direction. She had hardly any shoulders at all. The width of the shoulders should balance pleasingly with the width of the head and neck. This

63

woman had on a sweater which emphasized her problem. What could she do to correct her figure flaw? Puffed sleeves that stand out from the outside edge of the shoulder would be a help. Also yokes, wide necklines and lapels, cap sleeves and wide collars. Capes that are sewn over the upper garment and short sleeves with very wide cuffs would be good. Any sloping shoulder lines should be avoided, such as raglan sleeves and halters that expose the entire shoulder.

Wide Shoulders. All emphasis in the clothing should be taken away from the shoulder area. The reverse from above should be considered as good choices, also raglan sleeves, sleeves without shoulder fullness, V necklines (depending on face shape) narrow lapels and no padded shoulders. Choose vertical lines at the center front of the bodice and no horizontal lines of any kind going across the shoulders.

Flat Chested. No tight fitting sweaters, please. Choose things that have bodice fullness and bib effects, gathers, ruffles, tuckings, neckline bows and empire styles. Crisper fabrics will add fullness. Undies should have fullness and gathers at the bust to add fullness to the clothing on top. Last but not least, a padded bra will provide some fullness and make you much happier with your appearance in your clothing.

Protruding Tummy. Keep fullness at the stomach area. Jackets, peplums and tunics, when in style, help. A vest worn open over your blouse and skirt can be effective. Easy skirts and bloused above the waist tops are good. Accent your beautiful face with cosmetic color and keep interest high in your costume, close to the face.

Heavy Legs. A slight fullness at the hemline is much more flattering than a straight skirt. There should be no shine in the skirt fabric to call attention to the legs. Wear the skirts as long as you possibly can to be fashionable and keep lots of fullness in shorts or slacks. Darker colors in the panty hose, but in your Season, please!

Thin Legs. Here we can use the straight or slightly flared skirt to advantage. Area around the hemline should be a smaller area in keeping with smaller legs. Lighter shades of panty hose make the legs look larger.

CHOOSING CLOTHING TO SUIT YOUR SEASON

Your own personal color design is extremely important in knowing just which colors to build your wardrobe around. I will not go into great detail about this, but ask you instead to refer back to the chapters concerning wardrobe in **Color Me A Season** How to Find and Use Your Most Flattering Colors.

If we always consider our own Season's colors and the rules governing color choice for our complexion type, we cannot go far wrong.

There are numerous art texts that will show you how to put colors together in a pleasing combination. You might even want to purchase a Munsell® or a Prang® color wheel that will help you with your color bouquet choices.

The right line and design of clothing can be ruined if the color has been chosen incorrectly. Study carefully and you will become more expert at being your own fashion coordinator.

HOW TO USE THE "COLOR ME A SEASON COLOR FAN"

I created a color fan to help you extend your sixteen bouquet of colors to other shades and tints which will be attractive on you.

The fabric swatch packet containing your sixteen most attractive colors may be all you will need to pick and choose color for yourself. If you can see that a lighter color is a tint of one of your bouquet colors, then you have a good eye for color. The color fan is a visual aid to help you see the entire color spectrum placed into the four areas which we call Seasons.

The color fan is divided into four parts (all on one ring). Each section is identified as follows . . .

Summer's color bouquet is quiet with blue undertone. The darkest tint appears at the top of the color strip. It is shown in degrees of light and darkness that will be good for a delicate complexion type. For additional colors, use some of the tints (pastels) of Winter's dark shades. Combine Winter's red, white and blue for a Summer look. Winter's colors in light tints may also be used.

Winter's colors are blue undertoned in darker contrasting shades. For most effective use, wear only two shades at a time. The tints (pastels) of your bouquet may be worn in smaller areas or in a monochromatic color scheme. Darker shades of Summer colors might also be used, but should be checked with your complexion type.

Spring colors appear in their brightest intensity at the top of the strip. The lighter tints may also be attractive according to the intensity of complexion. A "Pastel Spring" may use the lightest tints, but may also use those of high intensity when correct cosmetic colors are worn. Some of Autumn's bouquet may be used if there is enough yellow or bright tone.

Autumn colors may be used in wide array from darks to light in monochromatic color schemes to contrast and blend with other colors of the bouquet. An Autumn person with very light complexion may use the very lightest tints of the bouquet and some of the darker shades when wearing the correct cosmetic colors.

PICKING YOUR COLORS FROM THE FAN

Spread out the entire color fan and find your area of color. In front of a well lighted mirror, hold up each individual strip of your bouquet of colors. Close one eye and run the strip under your chin. Observe each color as it passes. When you reach a color that begins to wash you out or one that seems too harsh for you, then mark a small x on the square to indicate it as an unusable color.

After you have gone through your entire color bouquet then check your corresponding bouquet. Summer-Winter, Spring-Autumn.

You may find a few useable colors from your corresponding

Season. Do not use any from the opposite side. These will be useful to you in determining if a material or piece of clothing is in the wrong color to suit your Season.

SHOPPING WITH THE FAN

You now have a fabulous aid in building your wardrobe, choosing jewelry, eyeglass frames, even paints to use in your interior decorating. You might even want to get that new car you are planning to buy in a color that fits you perfectly.

Hold your fabric choice or the color from the fan up to whatever you purchase to see if it is the right color range. If it seems a little wrong, check with the other Season's colors to see if it appears in an opposite bouquet.

Color memory is very short. Most people remember an exact color for only thirty minutes. After you have done a lot of shopping with your color aids, you may begin to remember your bouquet colors without any help. Wherever possible hold up a piece of clothing to your face and look in a mirror before purchasing. If it is a small item, check it to the skin tone on your hand.

To purchase paint, hold up your desired color to those on the store's display of paint chips. Match as closely as possible.

Let us review for a moment . . . We have gone into the areas that are important in choosing color for a more individualistic approach.
1. Lifestyle — our need for specific items of clothing
2. Age and personality type
3. Economic situation
4. Figure type
5. Season — your personal color design

GETTING READY FOR A NEW WARDROBE

Before I go into some actual ideas for wardrobe, it would be a good idea to study your closet where you keep all those valuable clothing items that you can't part with.

I know you are just like me. I have dresses in there that I can't bear to give away because they are like old friends. They remind me of past (slimmer) days: the material is so good, how could I possibly part with it. If I keep it long enough it will be in style again . . . Let's get that idea clarified.

Even though a style may come back in, say, twenty years from now, you will find subtle differences, either in the skirt or shoulder paddings or something that will make it still seem unfashionable. Materials age and get a mustiness to them. Our bodies, even though possibly the same weight, actually do change dimensions. It really won't look as good as it did the first time around.

If you have room and a place to store such memorabilia in a trunk or box that can be fumigated for moths, etc., than I do encourage you to keep some, NOT ALL, of your favorite clothes that have special meaning to you.

I have my pink prom dress from the 40's and my baby dress that mother saved for me. I don't have my wedding outfit because I wore it out. I opted for a suit instead of a white gown which I've been sorry for since.

I haven't been much of a saver of baby clothes and things for my children. I wish I had been more thoughtful.

That should show you that once in a while I do get a weeding out spree. That is what you need to do, either store it away somewhere else if you don't wear it, or better yet, give it away if it can be useful to someone else. Don't wait to give something away until it is terribly out of style. If you have clothing items in your closet that you do not use, or intend to use, then why not bless someone else with it while it is still usable.

Giving away clothing is a very touchy thing. Some people do not like to receive hand-me-downs and others love them. Be very sure that the recipient won't feel obligated to wear it even if they don't like it.

There are so many goodwill places now that would be happy to take things off your hands and you can deduct them from your taxes.

Another good place for good and usable clothing is a discount store that will sell your clothing for you and take a percentage of the cost. That might be a nice way to do it and you will feel better about getting rid of some of your clothing that you no longer wear.

On closet cleaning day, take each thing out one at a time and evaluate by the following questions:

1. Do I wear this?
2. Do I feel good in it when I wear it?
3. Is this the right line and design for me? Try it on if you have doubts and be very critical from all viewpoints.
4. Is this the right color for me? If not, is there some way I can put my right color with it to get more wear out of it?
5. Does this coordinate with any other piece of clothing in my closet? If so, put it with that area of clothing.
6. Is this still fashionable or basic in design?
7. If this is torn or worn, can I fix it up? Will I do it?

If a garment passes this test, then keep it in your closet, sorting out by putting all blouses together, all skirts in another section, dresses in another or . . . store by color families such as, all black items together with the blouses and coordinates that can be put together for an outfit.

Now go through your shoes, handbags, scarves and accessories and ask the same questions. Weed them out. Put away any savable items and arrange the floor of your closet neatly with just the shoes you really can wear.

Clean out your jewelry box and keep only those wearable pieces at hand to help you choose quickly when you need to. No more hunting around in the box for a lost earring. Keep all valuable items that you don't wear, but feel are worth something, in your safe deposit box or another box somewhere stored away.

Hang up your scarves and accessories neatly or fold them away in a special drawer, keeping only those things that you will use for sure.

If you have any maybe items, keep them in another spot that is handy and if you find you never use an item, then it belongs in your memory box or at the goodwill.

After this inventory, you are ready to start to build a new

wardrobe. I hope you have kept something and not wildly used this as an excuse to get everything new. I am a thrifty soul and I think you should use what you have if at all possible. I am not throwing out my fake fur cape, by the way. Even if it costs my husband some theater tickets in San Francisco, I'm going to wear that cape somewhere.

The following wardrobe plans are just that — plans. How could I ever choose your clothing for you? As an individual, you and only you know what you need in the way of clothing and I hope after reading this booklet you are ready to make some choices. Don't try to purchase everything at first, but choose only those items you need badly. Get your basic items and then add second choice blouses, accessories, etc.

WORKING A WARDROBE PLAN

Before making your first purchase you might want to sit down and study the WARDROBE AND COLOR PLANNER illustrated on pages 34 and 35. On a separate sheet of paper, write down all the clothing items you already have on this chart.

The pictures on the chart are only illustrations and represent the clothing items, not particularly the style **you** should wear. From what has already been discussed about your own personal lifestyle and needs, you will add to or eliminate items of clothing you wouldn't need or use.

Let's start from the beginning as if you were destitute of clothing and needed to purchase an entire wardrobe.

A wise start would be a jacket, skirt, slacks and vest all in the same color. With this you will need a blouse. (We will discuss color choices later). You now have the makings of eight clothing outfits.

With the addition of just one more blouse, you double your outfits to sixteen. This is getting exciting! Don't let me get ahead of myself. Your first choices were in what you consider to be your most flattering neutral color. Neutrals are considered black, brown, navy, beige, off-whites, whites, and gray.

DARKENED COMPLEXION COLOR A GOOD BASIC

The color of your skin is a good choice of color for yourself.

70

After all, God put you in that color and coded everything around it. You might choose that special blouse in the beige that most matches your skin tone or lighter.

Summer and Winter will be gray or pink beiges.

Autumn and Spring will be yellow beige or tans.

A Winter person needs to stay away from her beige for much of anything in her costume because it adds no contrast for that Winter design. She should choose instead, stark white.

If you will firmly pinch the end of your finger, you will find your dark complexion shade. This is very complimentary because it goes with your lighter skin tone. This sometimes is a very good color to use as a second choice neutral color as long as it will blend or go with the first neutral.

A neutral is a very quiet background color that many other colors can be used with. You would not want to choose a bright red for your basic mix and match outfits because both you and those around you would soon tire of seeing you in that color and remember it every time you appeared in the same suit or coat.

My own choice for the first four items is black because that is a very good color for me. As a Winter, I will have to consider that as my first neutral, but count it as one color choice. Those of you of the other three Seasons may use two or three other colors with your neutrals while Winters must use only two color choices to keep from being too busy. You can use more, but it is definitely better to keep your clothing simple.

My second choice is gray for the second set of jacket, skirt and slacks. I can use all of my bouquet colors with black and with gray and both of them will blend so that the gray jacket can be worn with black slacks, etc., etc.

Look at the first and second choice neutral color clothing and the blouse you want to get in your beige color that matches your complexion (choose white if you are Winter). Try to count the many changes this gives you. I count with one blouse over twenty changes and with two blouses, imagine all the mix and match combinations you will come up with.

We are dealing here with just three colors; neutrals at that. If you have chosen a shade that is very near your own skin tone,

71

WARDROBE AND COLOR PLANNER

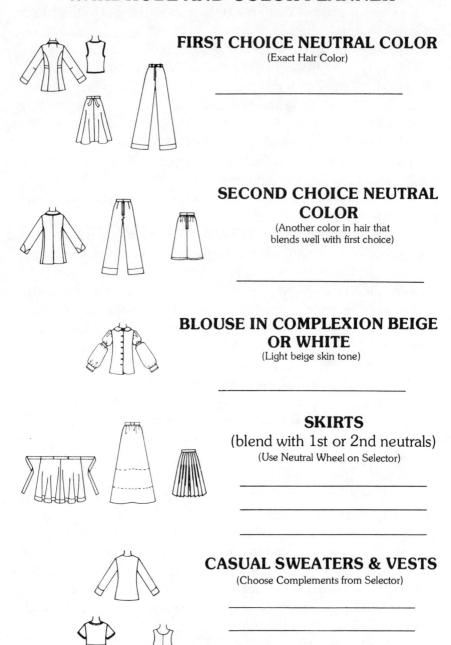

FIRST CHOICE NEUTRAL COLOR
(Exact Hair Color)

_____

SECOND CHOICE NEUTRAL COLOR
(Another color in hair that blends well with first choice)

_____

BLOUSE IN COMPLEXION BEIGE OR WHITE
(Light beige skin tone)

_____

SKIRTS
(blend with 1st or 2nd neutrals)
(Use Neutral Wheel on Selector)

_____
_____
_____

CASUAL SWEATERS & VESTS
(Choose Complements from Selector)

_____
_____
_____

BLOUSES IN CHOICE BOUQUET COLORS
(Find on Color Selector©)

1st _____

2nd _____

3rd _____

4th _____

DRESSES AS NEEDED
(Pinched Finger Red)

_____

_____

(Pink in Lower Lip)

DRESS IN MOST COMPLIMENTARY COLOR

_____

(Overall Eye Color)

ACCESSORIES & SHOES
(Match 1st and 2nd Neutral)

1st _____

2nd _____

Use your color fan to shop with and the color selector wheel for your season to get good ideas of putting colors together.

then you need to add some pizzaz to your costume. This is done by using jewlery, scarves, and various accessories. So far your clothing is very conservative no matter what Season you are. This is perfectly all right for business and more serious occasions, but one needs to add other colors from your color bouquet to sparkle up your wardrobe.

Looking at your bouquet colors, choose three or four that you like best and add blouses to go with your neutral tones. The addition of two or three skirts will greatly add to your wardrobe. These should blend if possible with either first or second neutral colors or at least one. Skirts should be suitable for different occasions. If long skirts are in, then you need at least one. A casual tie-around would be good for fun or at-home wear. This is only if you really look good in this type of skirt. Don't buy any item of clothing that is on the wardrobe planner if it is not your style. If you don't look good in suits, then substitute perhaps a jumper and jacket or basic dress with a jacket. If jackets aren't your best, then choose a sweater. In other words, the planner has been created to help you put together your perfect clothing for yourself. It should fit you and your individual style as we have covered previously.

Casual sweaters and vests are usually quite inexpensive and can add versatility to your clothing choices. Try wearing your cotton knit shirt over a complimenting blouse in a plaid or print. This gives a layered look as will vests. A shirt worn open over another shirt is something that can look a little different and add another clothing choice with skirt or slacks.

Dresses will have to be chosen as needed. You are the judge of how many you need. Generally it is fun to use some of your favorite colors that you wouldn't ordinarily use for suits or other things. If a dress has to be worn often, a more basic style and color will be better because anything unusual will stick in other people's minds and they will remember you wearing the same dress time and again.

A basic color or a neutral tone in a dress can be changed by adding different colored accessories and jewelry. If you are a dress person, then put your dresses up in the first and second neutral color choices.

When you need a dress for a very special occasion, it should be chosen in your very most complimentary color. Often times this will be the same color as your eyes or something that is complimentary to them. If hair coloring is unusually pretty, a matching dress can be very striking. Here again a complimentary color scheme can be very effective. Imagine a redheaded Autumn in a steel blue or aqua dress. Blue is complimentary to orange, which can be a terrific combination.

Accessory colors should match your first and second choice neutrals. If you choose these correctly, then one color of shoes should go with both shades.

A good rule is never wear a pair of shoes lighter than the hem of your skirt or slacks.

SHOES, PURSES AND ACCESSORIES

Personality enters a great deal in how many of each you need when it comes to purses, shoes and accessories.

I like a very simple look. Actually I would really like to load the jewelry on, but when I do, it looks garish on me (a Winter). I have to keep things simple in my clothing.

I love bright shiny patent purses and shoes, black of course, and plain leather dress-up shoes and purse in black. I know my failings and one of them is to forget something in my other purse, so I now choose just one handbag of very good quality and use it with everything except for an evening bag for special occasions.

For sports events, etc., (which I don't attend very much anyway) I am really out of place in slacks and my basic black dress-up purse. I have had lots of purses in my closet, but I just don't take time to change them. This is my own personality quirk.

Shoes should be chosen that are very good quality and have a go anywhere look. There are a lot of sales for shoes where you can pick up some fun styles and things that are different and a bit faddish.

Rule of thumb here would be to always have a pair of shoes or two that can take you anywhere you need to go and not be noticeable. For fun get a few pairs that especially please you or that match a particular outfit.

A pair of good fitting slippers or comfortable casual shoes are a really good buy to slip into when you come home to relax for the evening. This gives your good shoes a chance to breath and your feet a rest. If possible, wear one pair of shoes one day, and another the next, letting the shoes have a good airing. They will last longer if you have two instead of one to wear all the time.

Shop the dime stores and bargain basements for fun accessories that might become dated after a time. You can only wear a bright red polka dotted scarf so many times before you and others around you get tired of seeing it. If you want accessories that can be used for a long time, you will find a more conservative pattern or color will make less of a statement and be more useful to you over a period of time.

CHANGING SEASONS WITH YOUR WARDROBE

By now you realize that the colors from your color bouquet should be worn all year round. Each of us have some dark and some light colors that we can use. As the fashion industry recognizes Season's types we will begin to see our colors all year round. Until then, we have to take advantage of changes in fabric to make a wardrobe compatible with the weather.

Why should you give in to changing your Season's colors four times of the year? If you will shop carefully, you will find your colors out there but it may take some searching and smart shopping to do it.

The wardrobe planner will have to include both summer and winter clothing (seasons of the year, that is). You will need a coat for winter and one for summer, or a light jacket. These should be chosen in either your first or second choice neutral colors. You might enjoy a coat in a basic color rather than a neutral. A basic would be a color from your bouquet that will blend well with some of the other colors; blue, for instance, or green. Even red can be considered a basic color if you have enough things in your closet that will match it.

Neutrals are less memorable, basic colors next. Outstanding shades such as bright purple or hot pink would not be a good

76

choice for a piece of clothing you want to wear a lot.

You will need summer, short sleeved blouses, or long sleeves in light cottons or blends.

Some of your skirts and slacks will work well for all times of the year. Wools and heavy tweeds will, of course, have to be reserved for cooler times of the year.

If your clothing budget is tight, then plan carefully to purchase your clothing in fabrics that can be worn year round. Here in California we can almost have just one basic wardrobe.

KEEPING A GOOD PERSPECTIVE

Planning a wardrobe and dressing right is important to our happiness. We need to build our self-confidence to be more effective in our daily living.

In keeping a good perspective, we want neither to be a clotheshorse or a Plain Jane. We want to stay within a clothing allowance, one that our economic situation can stand. A families' welfare should not be sacrificed for a fashion conscious woman. Neither should a wife and mother neglect herself to completely sacrifice for husband and children.

A family is happier when all the members in it feel good about themselves and their appearance.

Clothing has been given to us as a protection and as an adornment. There is no need to be poorly dressed when so many alternatives are given us. A smart woman will plan her wardrobe to fit her needs using imagination and skills to make do with what she has.

May you and your wardrobe be well Seasoned!

FIGURATIVELY SPEAKING

Because every beauty book has a chapter on diet, let me inject some information on the subject, too. Believe me, I wish that God had created all men equal and all women beautifully thin. Because He didn't, and we all come in packages just a little different from each other, we all have a yearning to have a figure just like someone else.

Usually, that thin person is right inside ourselves, but most of us haven't the desire or ability to get that in our minds. We feel fat, even when we are thin.

I, personally, was born at 111 pounds. At least that is the weight that sticks in my mind. The teacher of our fifth grade class loudly proclaimed my weight to the whole class during a health weigh-in day. Of course, all the other girls were about 74 pounds. The fact that I had about reached my height of 5' 4" and all the other girls were still short didn't make any difference. I felt fat and ugly.

Horrible experiences like that have not made diets my favorite subject. I have been on every one invented and my file bulges with *thin* plans.

Fat is a matter of attitude. I have seen extremely thin people who feel they are horribly fat. On the other hand, there are some heavy people who don't mind their size at all.

Discovering my Season has helped me a great deal because it really is true that when you wear the proper colors, people look more at your beautiful face than they do your body.

Learning some of those tricks in the section on Fashion Line and Design has also helped me feel better about myself.

There are just some times in your life, though, that a period of eating less is necessary. Aren't you like me? We just need one negative comment or look in the mirror to know the time has come to get with it and get it off.

Some helpful programs for me have been Weight Watchers, The Diet Center, and Thin Within. All of them have supportive group plans.

I once reached my goal weight at a local health spa on the exercise diet routine. My figure never looked better.

All of these programs and more are excellent to get the weight off.

I like the Thin Within program because it helped me finally see the thin person inside myself.

One of my favorite church authors, Sterling W. Sill, has written about the *As If* principle. That really works well, too. If you act like a thin person, you will become one. Remember, though, each of us has a different image of what thin is. Mine is somewhere at the romantic figure type—a little soft and curvy. For me that is how I feel best. I really can't get excited about bony arms and legs. On other people they look great, but my inside spirit person feels softer, and so I can be satisfied with a little more weight than others might think is right for me.

We have to like ourselves. We are the ones we need to please. Our bodies are such personal things. Dieting is really our own business.

Now, I do think that there is a point beyond our own personal image that our being overweight begins to affect other people and also interferes with our success in life.

Our families need to be proud of us, and our appearance can make a big difference on the job, so----

Why not try again if your weight is making you unhappy and unsuccessful?

For one of our COLOR YOU FASCINATING classes for teen girls I had the challenge of coming up with a good diet plan that was nutritionally sound but fun enough for teen girls to stay on and have some degree of success.

The YUMMY MONEY diet was born. It has been successful for those who want a fun, new approach to keeping track of what they are eating during the day. It is designed for men, women, and children.

I cannot include it in this book because it is a large packet of food money that you can spend throughout the day and forget the calorie counting. It has worked for me in the past and made it easier to get a well balanced diet that allows enough food to make you feel that you are not fasting to lose weight.

It also puts a little sense of humor into a rather boring process.

We have advertised it nationally at $7.95, but if you would like the diet you may order it for $4.95 and $1.00 for postage. Ask for the Diet Money and mail it to:

COLOR ME A SEASON
P.O. Box 864
Concord, CA 94519

I certainly would love to hear from you later to see how successful you have been with it and perhaps a before-and-after photo that could be shared with others. Also, any fun recipes that you create for the diet that can help the rest of us would be appreciated.

I could give you some other diets that have worked for me such as my Cottage Cheese and Applesauce and That's All Diet. The Meat Fruit and Vegetable Diet did a good job for me, but I really don't feel good about the nutritional aspects of such diets.

Another really good source of diet information is your Agricultural Extension Bureau. They usually have excellent diet plans.

Practically every magazine you pick up has a new diet plan for you to try. The sources are there, The incentive to do it is within yourself.

YOUR CROWNING GLORY

Hair Care and Styling for the Seasons

In my color classes I spend about three hours teaching about color, doing Seasons for each individual and then going into a complete cosmetic analysis so the colors on each person are perfect from head to toe.

Many times I am anxious to get into the hair coloring and styling, but time does not permit. It is with this in mind that I go into this booklet to help you obtain a real CROWNING GLORY for yourself so you truly will be correct in styling and color from the crown of your head to the tips of your toes.

In **"Color Me A Season"** I mentioned the right colors of hair for each Season and I hope that was helpful to you. I will now attempt to help you more with not only coloring for your hair, but hair care itself. We will also go into care of hair all over your body, find out its purpose and how to take care of it.

WHAT IS HAIR?

The technical definition of hair is an appendage or modification of the skin. It is constructed of layers of cells over a medulla (center or pith) with scale-like formations on the outer surface.

These little scales are like the shingles on a roof. They overlap each other. It is important to understand this construction because later we will be talking about hair products that are applied to the hair, and knowing that you are dealing with a scaly surface will be important to you.

It is also important to understand the construction of a hair and how it is fed so you won't be confused by certain claims made by different companies on how their products feed and help the hair.

Let's delve into the construction of hair a little more.

81

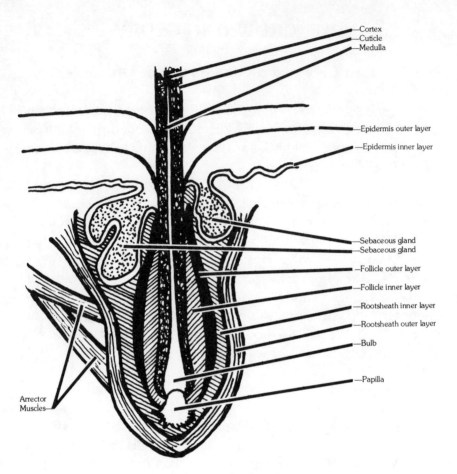

Cortex
Cuticle
Medulla

Epidermis outer layer

Epidermis inner layer

Sebaceous gland
Sebaceous gland
Follicle outer layer
Follicle inner layer
Rootsheath inner layer
Rootsheath outer layer
Bulb
Papilla

Arrector
Muscles

Longitudinal Cross Section

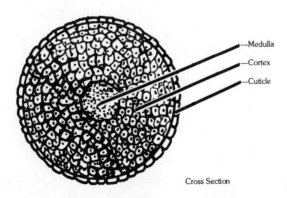

Medulla
Cortex
Cuticle

Cross Section

82

1. The cuticle - Outer layer of delicate, scale or scale-like cells which overlap as explained before.

2. The cortex - A middle portion which makes up the main part of the shaft, formed of long cells which give the hair flexibility. Small openings in the cortex hold the oil which gives hair its sheen. This layer also contains the pigment, which, showing through the outer horn, makes hair black, red, brown, yellow or the color of your Season.

3. Medulla - Inner layer formed of round cells (the pith or center) of the hair. The short, fine hairs on the surface of the body do not have this layer, and sometimes it is absent from long, coarse hair.

4. The shaft or stem - The part that projects above the skin.

5. The bulb - At the end of the hair is a rounded portion that is sometimes mistakingly called the root. It is composed of soft growing cells and fits into an opening in the skin called the follicle.

Now this takes care of the construction of the hair itself. So how does it attach itself to the body and how is it fed?

1. The follicle is the tube-like opening in the skin through which the hair grows and reaches the surface. It holds the hair into the skin. It is with some effort that one pulls the bulb of the hair through the follicle to remove it from the body.

It is a good thing that this fitting is as tight as it is or we would be losing more of our hair all the time than we already do.

2. The papilla is situated at the bottom of the follicle and fits up closely to the hair bulb. It is a cone-shaped formation that has nerves and blood vessels which furnish the hair with nourishment. The hair does not really have roots that attach to the body in any way. The bulb of the hair absorbs into itself the food from the papilla.

When someone tells you that putting something on the hair itself will feed it and nourish it, take a second look at that product.

Because, the hair receives no nourishment at all from an outside source, other than the papilla which is affected by our nerves and blood supply.

Hair cosmetics and conditioners may soften or smooth the scales on the hair shaft or build it up with protein deposits, etc. Therefore, one might say the hair has been helped, but not fed.

OTHER THINGS THAT AFFECT THE HAIR FORMATION

Two other things affect the hair.

1. The erector pili muscle which is located in the second layer of the skin is connected to the hair. When this muscle contracts the follicle in which the hair shaft is contained, the muscle pulls the hair into a direction or makes it, so to speak, stand on end.

2. The sebaceous glands supply the hair with natural oil and are located near the surface or skin of the scalp. They open into the hair follicle. Any stimulation of the sebaceous glands makes them secrete more oil.

Brushing the hair 100 strokes a night used to be a method suggested for helping the hair grow.

You can brush your hair that much if you want to, to stimulate the blood supply. But I think holding your head down, forcing more blood into the vessels, while brushing, is actually what helps feed the hair. Brushing usually brings the oil from the sebaceous glands out further onto the hair's surface and unless you wash often, you will find this makes your hair more oily than you might like it to be.

Massaging the scalp with a firm motion with fingertips or a mechanical massager will do more to feed the hair than brushing will.

You must be very careful in choosing the hair brushes and combs you use on your hair, for they may be the cause of breaking your hair. The new plastic brushes are so inexpensive, but be careful to get one that does not cause split hairs. Combs, too, will break your hair. A hard rubber comb is preferable to plastic if you can find one.

WHAT CAUSES HAIR TO FALL OUT

If you are being really careful with your hair to keep it from breaking and it is still coming out abnormally, it may be due to a disfunction of the nerves and blood supply through the papilla. The health of your hair depends upon the health of the body. If you are not in good health, your hair will show it.

A friend of mine did a complete turnabout from mousey, lackluster hair to beautiful thick hair which was shiny and pretty. Her hair had, for years, been falling out and looking really bad when she found that she needed a complete historectomy which had been causing a great deal of blood loss and anemia in her body.

I did not see her for about six months after her operation and was amazed at the difference in her hair.

The blood is the food supply of the hair and scalp. When poisons are brought to the hair structure by way of the blood, the hair suffers.

If you have ever had anesthesia, you may notice that for several weeks afterwards you will lose a lot of hair. This is because toxin has entered into the blood and has affected the papilla nerves. Usually they recover and all is well again.

This is the reason it is better to put off having a permanent wave or hair tint for a few weeks after surgery because the scalp is in a weakened condition from the operation.

This used to be an even bigger problem than it is today with our modern methods of feeding the body intravenously while recovering from an operation.

If there is any disturbance in the metabolism or in the glands of internal secretion it may result in changes of the hair. Anything that affects the quality and quantity of the blood affects hair growth.

My mother-in-law had the most gorgeous white hair one could imagine. When she was about thirty-five years old she contracted scarlet fever. During her illness every bit of her dark brown hair came out. When it came back in, it was snow white.

People who have been through a severe shock of any kind

85

may notice a definite change in the hair.

HOW MANY HAIRS ARE ON OUR HEAD

A normal head of hair contains about 120,000 hairs. These vary from person to person and each of us has our own pattern of hair growth as we do other patterns and designs of the body.

Hairs are coming and going all of the time. The normal life of a hair is two to four years. Then it reaches its full potential, the ends split and then break off.

Have you ever noticed times when you have more split hairs than others? It is entirely possible that you may have had a new growth of these same hairs a few years back and they have reached their growth potential all at the same time.

Eyelashes last from three to five months. They fall out and are replaced one at a time so that we aren't devoid of eyelashes all at once.

Hair on our head grows about one-half inch a month. It grows more rapidly in summer than in the winter. Pulling out the hair does not increase the growth rate nor does shaving the legs increase the hairs on the leg surface. When you cut or pull the hairs it does allow those in other follicles around it to grow faster, therefore, you may feel it has increased hair growth.

There are many more hair follicles on the surface of the skin than there are any hairs. As a person ages we may see more hairs growing on previously non-hairy surfaces.

WHAT GIVES HAIR ITS COLOR

You are going to be amazed that just as your eyes have a design or color pattern, so does your own particular hair.

This chart will show you how four different persons' hair patterns, for coloring, look as seen through a microscope.

Just as in the entire skin surface, we find that melanin and keratin are important to the coloring of the hair.

Keratin is the substance of all horny outgrowths of the skin, such as nails, and hair. On animals it forms hoofs, horns and

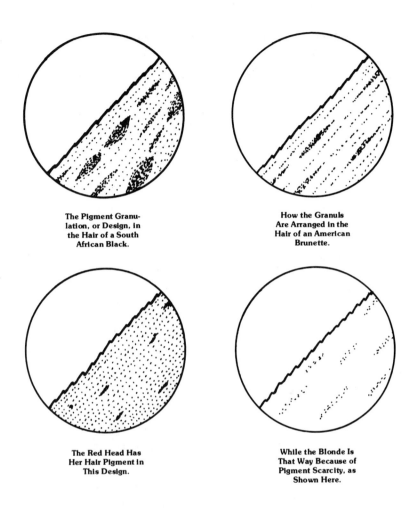

The Pigment Granu-
lation, or Design, in
the Hair of a South
African Black.

How the Granuls
Are Arranged in the
Hair of an American
Brunette.

The Red Head Has
Her Hair Pigment in
This Design.

While the Blonde Is
That Way Because of
Pigment Scarcity, as
Shown Here.

feathers.

The malanin (Greek word for black) is the coloring matter of hair. These chemical elements combine to make up a hair.

Carbon	44%
Hydrogen	6%
Nitrogen	15%
Oxygen	30%
Sulphur	5%

These chemicals are found in different proportions in different colors of hair. Here again another genetic factor that goes into making up your own personal color design.

Light hair contains less carbon and hydrogen and more oxygen and sulphur.

Dark hair contains more carbon and less oxygen and sulphur.

HAIR SHAPES

Your hair not only has a design for coloring, it also has a shape. Straight hair is round. Wavy is oval. Curly hair is flat.

IMPORTANCE OF KNOWING SCIENTIFIC FACTS

I have found that any time one knows a subject well, it serves to help care for that particular object; in this case our hair structure.

If you have been able to wade through this sifting of facts, then perhaps you will see that some product advertising is misleading.

Hair products, for instance, do not feed the hair and they cannot make the hair grow faster or produce any miracles.

There are some things that we can do to help stabilize and strengthen the hair shaft and make it more lustrous and attractive. Good hygienic hair care will do as much as anything to give you beautiful hair. Health care is another important factor. Perhaps a really good vitamin and mineral supplement, when suggested by your doctor, would be good for you.

THIN, WEAK HAIR

Although most of us have approximately 120,000 hairs on our head, some people do not seem to have a nice thick full head of hair.

Naturally, there are those who do not have this number of hairs. It is possible to have numerous hairs on the head, but the structure of the hair itself is very fine textured.

Other textures may be described as medium or coarse. It may

be very wiry or silky and may have a harsh or soft feeling.

In my days when doing hair styling, I had ladies who would come in with a picture of a desired hairstyle. Most of them did not realize that their own hair texture was not the same as on the model pictured. They usually were very pleased to have me create their very own personal hair style suited just for them.

OTHER HAIR ON THE BODY

Before we go further on hair care, we need to be aware that much of our body has hair on it called lanugo. Before you were born you were covered with this fine downy fuzz. The body sheds most of this covering of hair before birth but we still retain hair all over the body with the exception of the palms of the hands and the soles of the feet.

The hair that is left on the body is very fine and unnoticeable except for eyebrows, eyelashes, whiskers, and heavier hair found on legs and underarms.

We don't have to worry about this hair growth, but, we do need to keep ourselves well-groomed by shaving legs and underarms and if a man, shaving the whiskers.

The facial hair is called cilia and it covers the face and is useful to us if we apply our makeup and then seal it with a fine film of face powder. The powder is applied with soft downward strokes to make the cilia lie down. To keep the face natural and unpowdered looking, you need only to touch the powder with a damp sponge or cotton ball to bring up the shine and leave the set.

TWEEZING EYEBROWS

Your eyes are your most beautiful feature, or at least can be, with proper colors on your body and in your cosmetic colors. They need a frame, just as a picture does. Your eyebrows and eyelashes serve to keep dirt and debris out of the eye, but they also frame the eye in a pretty arch.

Eyelashes take care of themselves as they grow for three or four months and fall out, being replaced by another lash. Eyebrows hang in there a little longer and sometimes grow where we do not want them to.

To tweeze your brows perfectly, follow the natural shape and tweeze all strays out from under the brow. Follow this procedure:

1. Look in the mirror to determine how your brows look. Are they in good basic shape? Are they really heavy and unruly? If you really have a problem, find a beautician who does brows and get your first tweezing done professionally. Or choose a friend who really knows how to do her own brows well and ask her to help you tweeze yours.

2. Take an old toothbrush or an eyebrow brush and brush all the hairs upwards. Then, smooth your finger along the top of the brow from the bridge of the nose to the end of the brow. You may find this is all you need. I hope you will get in the habit of brushing your brows every day to train them to lie in a smooth line.

3. Draw an imaginary line from the end of your eye, nearest your nose, up to your hairline. Any hairs that are in the area between your nose need to come out. If your brows don't come to this point then you need to use *Brush On Brow* to fill out for a perfect framing.

4. Wrap an ice cube in a cloth and hold it on the side of your face where you will begin tweezing. Hold this on your brow for a good five minutes. This will deaden the area for painfree tweezing. You may use rubbing alcohol on a cotton ball. Swab over the area and then begin to tweeze immediately.

5. Grab the hair to be tweezed by the end and pull it out in the direction it is growing. Fast pulling will make the job easier. Go immediately to another hair and practice at pulling quickly. (Try to find a tweezer that has a scissor type handle. The ones that pinch together with a wide tweezing head are not good and are the reason for failing to do a good job.) Go to your local beauty supply to purchase a professional tweezer. This is a tool you will use a lot so don't scrimp on this. Completely tweeze out all the hairs that lie under the smooth line of your brow. Do not go above to tweeze hairs, but if you find one of those longies that is growing wild, pull it out too.

6. Apply the alcohol anytime it begins to hurt and when the job is completed. Use the ice cube again or a cold wash cloth to make your brows feel better.

7. Wait for the red to subside before applying makeup.

Wax Dipilatories

You might want to use the wax kind of hair removers on the eyebrows, but be extremely careful not to get it on any hair you do not want to remove. This depilatory is bees wax which is very hard when it is cool. To remove, rip the wax off after it has hardened in the direction the hair is growing. This is so much more painful than tweezing I don't think you should try it all at one time. Test on a tiny area before you do your entire brow areas.

Bees wax is also used to remove hair on other parts of the body. It is effective, but not quite as comfortable as other methods.

ABSOLUTELY, DO NOT USE CHEMICAL DEPILATORIES ON THE EYE BROWS. Even though this product is effective on other areas of the body, it might drip or splash into the eye. The result of course could be very harmful to the eyes.

Chemical depilatories will remove hair from underarms and legs. These products are composed of thioglycolic acid, chalk, wax and water. The acid weakens the hair so it will break off. The hair comes off at skin level or slightly below.

The drawback to this product is that it can cause an irritation to the skin.

SHAVING

The quickest and most painless way to remove hair from legs and underarms is of course, shaving. Be sure to use a good lather of soap or shaving cream. This will help you get a better cut and your skin will not be scraped from the razor.

The only reason hair looks blacker after shaving is that the ends of the hair are cut off blunt and they seem coarser. When you pull hairs out one by one, or by waxing, you remove the bulb of the hair. When the new hair forms it comes out with a fine point instead of a blunt cut. Therefore, the hair does not seem so much like whiskers when they start to grow in.

ELECTROLYSIS AS HAIR REMOVAL

Sometimes hair is such a problem on the face that it needs more professional help. It is expensive, but is a good way to remove unsightly facial hair. BE VERY SURE OF THE PERSON WHO DOES THE HAIR REMOVAL. I have seen ugly scars from electrolysis by an unskilled person. Get some recommendations from other people who have had it done first.

Electrolysis is a long process but effective because the hair bulb and papilla are destroyed so no hairs can be grown out of the follicle.

Removing hair with the hot wax treatment also will destroy some of the hair growth centers (the papilla).

It is very necessary to good grooming to keep unwanted hair off the body. Shaving underarms will help to eliminate some body odor. The hair in the armpits holds in perspiration. A deordorant will work more effectively when the hair is removed.

Deodorant should not be applied to freshly shaved areas. Sometimes I use some scented talcum powder immediately after shaving which is not only soothing, but serves to make up for deodorant until the next day when I can apply deodorant again. Arms can become extremely irritated if you apply deodorant when the skin has been scraped. Be sure to check on your deodorant bottle to see if it is safe to apply after shaving.

All of this may seem very removed from hair styling for your Season, but it is all part of caring for the hair on our bodies. We want to be perfect in our Season and we need to care for our bodies all over rather than just concentrating on our face and head.

HAIRCOLOR AND YOUR SEASON

Do you really need to change the color of your hair? Probably not. Have you tried wearing your pretty bouquet colors for your Season, especially with your correct cosmetic shades?

During a personal color analysis of one Autumn individual, the hair color changed from mousey brown to a metallic sheen of golden brown. The transformation was so noticeable it drew a gasp of astonishment from her.

With her pretty cosmetics applied properly and draped in Autumn colors, this woman, who would have been described as quite plain and ordinary, transformed into a lovely lady.

Let me tell you a secret. . . Hardly anyone is a raving beauty in the complete natural form. It is like your garden. You have to keep the weeds out of it and groom it, bordering it with pretty flowers and shrubs. If you will spend some time on yourself each day, you will be as pretty as anyone else.

If you have done everything you can with color and cosmetics and you still feel you need a change in hair coloring, then the instructions in **"Color Me A Season"** should be followed. I will repeat that information here.

Summer's hair shades should be soft and delicate. It is possible to have any shade and still be Summer. However, if your natural shade was never brunette, it would be better for you to stay within the blonde or brownette shades. Some lovely effects can be obtained by using blonde tints on greying hair.

Note: Choose hair coloring products in the ash tones.

Consider changing salt and pepper hair to a silver shade. Nature knows what it is doing when hair changes to silver in old age. White or silver hair softens facial features that have become harsh over the years. Silver hair can be very glamorous if set in a becoming new style.

I never encourage hair tinting with permanent tints unless the grey becomes impossible to cover with a temporary six-week product. Shop around before making a final decision to change your hair coloring. Remember, it takes a treatment every six weeks when you start tinting your hair. It is better never to start unless you are willing to stand the expense of keeping it looking nice.

Unless your hair is naturally red, do not go to any red, bronze, copper or similar color. If you are a natural redhead, the Summer colors will be becoming because your skin, eyes, and hair have been coordinated by nature. Others will have a hard time imitating a similar color scheme.

Springs, enhance your own hair shade with temporary rinses to bring out a sheen and a glow. Radiance is your Season, so hair that glistens will certainly enhance your appearance. Avoid a dull look for the hair. Try to achieve a brilliant look.

If hair is greying slightly, use blonde tones or brown to match your own shades. Keep color in your hair as long as possible. Grey hair gives more of a Summer or Winter look.

For grey that won't go away, use rinses or tints that give a lot of luster. You may, when hair is silver, be able to use a few more of Summer's color bouquet as long as you continue to use Spring's makeup.

Note — it is better when using pastels as a Spring person to be sure the colors have a yellow toned base. Example, pink — there are some pinks that have a bluish tint to them. Some pinks have a yellow base. For fun while you are in the fabric store hold up pinks to each other to see the blue or yellow in them. Use your fabric swatches and if possible use the color fan for your Season to help you *see* the pastels of your colors. The **"Color Me A Season"** colorfan will help you find your tints of your basic sixteen colors.

Redheaded Springs, keep your hair that shade as long as you can, or go to soft browns with hints of red or gold.

Autumns, try to get a coppery look to your hair. Keep hair in good condition with oil treatments to bring out luster. Dark auburn is lovely on an Autumn. Avoid a false red look. Orange tones in the hair will enhance your Season's color.

For light Autumns with blonde or light brown hair, stay to your own shades, perhaps with slight gold tints. A dark red on a fair Autumn can be very harsh looking. Remember, nature put you together in an original color scheme. Try to stay with it.

Keep grey out of the hair as long as possible because of the

Summer or Winter look it gives. When grey does take over, then keep it lustrous (no blue or ash tones, please). Continue to wear your color bouquet with a change in metals to silver, if it looks better on you.

Winters, when changing hair coloring, go to the ash tones which do not have red in them. Hair that is dark brown might be a little darker to give a more Wintery look. Stay basically with what you were born with.

Naturally redheaded Winters are rare, but when it happens, stay with that color because eyes and skintone will correspond. You might like to use a temporary dark auburn tint to bring out luster and deepen the color. Stay away from the bright red or oranges.

Blonde Winters might add a silver look to the hair tone. Light brown hair will benefit with slightly darker shade.

Greying hair should be controlled with temporary rinses or tinting until unusual effects of white begin (such as white streaks at the hairline or temples). These are dramatic and add to Winter's design.

Grey hair should be made to look as white or silver as possible. It is very becoming to the Season. Often very black hair will turn to a beautiful silver, early in life. Be glad for this and choose a becoming new style for the hair; it will add to your elegance.

FACTS ABOUT HAIR COLORING PRODUCTS

Before you make a final decision about changing the color of your hair, perhaps the following information will help you understand what you are doing to your hair when you color it. Then if the pros of having a nicer color outweigh the controversial effects of these chemicals on your hair, go ahead and make a change.

Fact number one. From the moment you apply a changing chemical on the hair, its effects will last at least three years. Remember that hair life is from two to three years and so even though you will lose many hairs before the three years are up, you will have some of them for the full three years as they are new hairs. Cutting the hair off short will probably take care of that problem if you decide to go back to your natural color.

It is possible to change the color of your hair and then have it restored to its original color if you are dissatisfied with what you have done, but the hair shaft has been damaged and will never be quite the same again.

Proper conditioners can be a help and you do have to be careful to use less harsh shampoos to avoid hair damage.

TYPES OF COLORING AVAILABLE

1. Color Rinses or non-permanent coloring

I remember experimenting with these hair rinses when my hair was pretty enough without them. We bought them in the five and dime in capsule form and mixed them with warm water and poured them through and through again until the water was clear. Then you knew that the hair had taken up all the color. At first it was marvelous to see yourself as a redhead or dark brunette. Then each time you slept on your pillow or combed your hair, a bit of the color would rub out. And, heaven forbid, if you went in swimming most of your tinting would come out in the water about your head, when it first got wet.

Some of these tints are contained in shampoo coloring products. They are a bit more lasting than the kind I used when I was a girl, but they still are very temporary and really only intended to enhance or highlight the hair.

2. Semi-permanent tints

These products do not contain peroxide, ammonia or chemicals that will soften the outside of the hair shaft to allow the color to soak in. They stay on the hair for a temporary time and each time the hair is shampooed, part of the coloring fades out or is washed away.

If your hair is just faded and you want to brighten it up, this is the tint you want. If your hair is starting to grey, but not severely so, then this will do the job of covering for a time.

After the hair becomes very grey, then semi-permanent tints are not satisfactory. You have to make the decision to let it go grey naturally, or tint with a more permanent solution.

3. Permanent tinting

These products contain either vegetable, metallic or aniline dyes. The best type is the aniline.

Henna

This is an example of a vegetable dye which coats the hair shaft. Improvements have been made in this product and today you can purchase henna that will give you colors other than red.

Once you have started to use henna, you may notice that your hair becomes dry and stiff. This is due to the coating or buildup on the hair shaft. As long as the henna remains on the hair, it will not take kindly to permanent waving or any kind of semi-permanent or permanent tinting. You must get rid of the henna completely to make changes in your hair. Time and patience will win out and eventually the henna will wear off. You may help the process along by shampooing with a strong shampoo that will strip the hair shaft, or by giving yourself a hot oil treatment.

Hot oil treatment

Heat a little olive oil in a cup and rub a little on the scalp. Part your hair and apply along the part. Continue parting off the hair and covering with oil until the entire scalp has been covered. Comb the oil out onto the hair and cover with a hot steam cap or hot towels for fifteen minutes. After the steaming, shampoo the hair thoroughly at least two sudsings with very warm water to remove the oil. This treatment will improve your hair anytime it has been damaged. It is also useful to loosen a permanent wave that has been too curly.

4. Metallic Dyes

These are sometimes called hair restorers. These are the kind that are applied by combing through the hair day after day until the hair begins to take on a darker color. The color is not pretty and shiny and your hair will become stiff and dry. Copper dies make red hair. Silver develops into a greenish color and lead will make a purple or blue cast. It is possible to get lead poisoning from this last dye and I feel it is not very wise to use this type of product.

A special remover must be used to take away the color from these dyes and they must not be in the hair when you do a permanent wave or another type of hair tint.

5. Aniline dyes

These are by far the most satisfactory of the permanent tints. There are thousands of different color possibilities with aniline dyes. The coloring agent actually enters the hair shaft and permanently colors the hair.

Since the color does not fade out, then special precautions must be made when coloring the new hair growth (about 6 weeks growth). The tint mixture must be applied at the scalp hair partings and after the prescribed time, combed out onto the ends of the hair to brighten up the coloring in the shaft that has dulled and faded a little.

This is a tedious routine, but if you can do it easily yourself you might not mind. If you can stand the expense of shop tints, then this is the best way to get a new colorful look to your hair.

Be careful to do the skin tests suggested because many people are allergic to aniline dyes. Be especially careful to avoid the eye areas with these tints.

DO NOT TINT EYELASHES OR BROWS WITH THEM.

You can do four types of coloring with aniline dyes:

1. Shampoo tints — slightly tints the cortex of the hair and needs refreshing every six weeks.

2. Shampoo-in-the dye penetrates deeper into the cortex. This must be shampooed in again in six weeks. No need to

part or section the hair.

3. One step processing—should be done professionally. The hair will need good reconditioners and special shampoos.

4. Two step processing—the most difficult of all to apply and re-apply. This should be done professionally. Hair may show a lot of breakage and damage in spite of conditioning.

FROSTING YOUR HAIR

There are do-it-yourself kits for frosting the hair, or you may get this done professionally in a salon. This will give a blonde look to brownette hair and is not particularly good on gray hair. This type of hair color change need only be done every two to four months. It seems more natural when it grows out.

WHICH COLOR TO CHOOSE

On most hair coloring packages you will find a chart that will tell you the color you are going to get if you use that particular shade. If your hair is light blonde, the color is going to turn out lighter and different than if your hair is very dark brown. These charts are quite accurate and should be paid attention to.

One little redhead that I knew decided that she just had to have brunette hair. Although she was advised against it, she impulsively had it tinted anyway. Her first mistake was to not recognize her golden red color design. You know what black does to a Spring person anyway. If you started out in life with dark black hair and you are a Spring, then God coded you that way and it is alright, but you just can't fake it with hair coloring and make that big a change from your own natural area of color.

The story ends on a very sad note. The next time I saw my little friend she had green black hair! She ended up going to a beauty salon and had to have all of the color stripped out of the hair and her own color, or close to it, put back in. She was lucky that it turned out just a little streaked. It is risky to fool around with hair dyes because they can really fool you.

Her hair was in bad condition for a long time, but she learned to leave that gorgeous red hair alone because it was so perfect for her in the first place.

I always feel a little conservative when using hair coloring from a chart and if it says it will be, for instance, medium brown when you are done, I figure on it being very dark brown.

When I want my hair to be dark brown, I choose a medium ash brown and even that is very dark if I leave it on too long. This makes me remind you to set a timer and be accurate in your application time. Be a little conservative there, too.

A good rule to remember is the first time you try it, go lighter, because you can always make it darker, but you can't make it lighter after it is processed.

Let me repeat again that if you are Summer or Winter you should have your hair done in quiet ash tones, platinum blondes (not golden), quiet reds (not brassy or bright).

If you are Spring or Autumn, choose golden blondes, red blondes, warm browns (instead of ash).

There are so few beauticians at this point who understand about the Seasons color concept, I would hesitate to have one choose color for you. This is where you will have to stand firm with your hairstylist and ask to see the color swatch chart they have for hair coloring to be sure you are going to get what you need for your Season. Do not listen to a wrong color concept about hair, but be firm in insisting on certain colors.

The one point that an experienced beautician who has worked a lot with hair tinting will know is . . . the color you are going to wind up with if you put a certain tint on your color of hair. Ask her / him to show you the color he/she is aiming for. Get out your color swatch packet or better yet, your color fan that has 216 colors and see if the red, browns or blacks or blondes go with the neutral colors of the same hue on the fan. If they match pretty well, then proceed with your changeover.

Just as with the cosmetics — if the color looks good on your body, it will look good on your face. The same applies to color for your hair.

PAY A VISIT TO THE WIG SALON

Before changing your hair coloring drastically, I would suggest going to your local wig salon and actually trying on the different colors. See how the colors look on you. Wear your correct cosmetic colors when you go and wear one of your neutrals out of your bouquet, or your best color. This could save you a tragic mistake. Observe very closely how the hair coloring effects your skin tone and if it washes you out or takes over your complexion color.

Take an honest friend with you when you go to help you decide. You will be glad you followed this advice if you turn out just beautiful in your new hair coloring.

You might even be satisfied to purchase the wig instead of doing the complete changeover on yourself.

AGE AND HAIRCOLORING

As you mature in years, your hair begins to turn silver. It is more becoming to the skin if it is wrinkled or less than perfect. The right cosmetic colors will help you wear your hair almost near the natural shade it has been all your life.

You might consider going a little bit lighter with your hair tints if your hair is almost fully grey. This might be the time to try being that glamorous blonde. Be sure though, that it is either ash or golden, depending on your Season. As you mature, do not go darker than your own natural color was with your hair coloring.

Many older women ask me if their Season changes when they get older. No, the Season does not change. Your hair may turn grey and the skin tone may become lighter or more sallow, but you are still the same in skin tone. Wearing the proper colors for your color design will help you retain a more youthful look all your life, regardless of your age.

CARE OF DYED OR TINTED HAIR

If you have taken the plunge and created a new color for your hair, you need to take care of it properly. If you don't, you will have color changes or even broken or damaged hair.

Easy does it, is a good rule. The hair has been weakened by chemicals and so be sure the shampoos and rinses or conditioners you use after tinting are compatible to your hair in its new state.

Look for qualities in buying shampoos that will not strip the hair of all its oil. You especially need to be careful if you tint your hair or have strong permanent waving often.

There are so many products on the market that it can be confusing to you. If you have professional help in coloring your hair the stylist will use proper products. If you don't, usually the coloring agent you use has a correct type of shampoo that can be used safely.

PERMANENTS — WHO NEEDS THEM?

You certainly don't, of course, right after a tint, but even then, if your hair is lifeless and needs body to retain a style, a perm is just the thing for you.

Give yourself a few weeks after a tint to wave your hair. Recondition it first with the Protein Hair Reconstructor by leaving in the final rinse for about an hour with a turban wrapped bath towel after your shampooing. Then rinse with tepid water.

If you are having a professional permanent, then rely on the experience of your beautician. Remember to tell her/him all the things you have done to your hair, or you may wind up with a surprise. It is very important to tell what hair tinting products you have used on your hair, so keep a diary of what was used and how long it has been since the last treatment. All these things will add to more beautiful hair for you in the long run.

I wear my hair in a soft, close to the head cut. Once in a while I go in to get a perm, but by the time my hair is cut, it lies so nicely that I usually come home without any permanent. If you get a really super cut, it is sometimes all that is needed to give body. I inherited a good thick head of hair from my Winter father. If it was thin and limp I would definitely resort to permanent waving. As long as it is short I don't need anything but a good set or blowdry to make it look good.

Most people only need a body perm. This is set on larger rods and for a shorter period of time. No longer is it fashionable to have tight tiny curls that are later set into a hairstyle.

Reserve the tight perms for the styles that are wash and wear just like the curls one of my daughters inherited naturally.

For years we fought with those curls trying straighteners and every method to get the kinks out. Now we just cut it short and let it curl into a darling hairstyle — just perfect for her Spring Season.

There are so many different types of lotions for permanents. I will leave it up to you to find the best one for yourself. If you don't get a professional wave, be sure the friend you choose to do it for you will do a good job. Read all the instructions and follow them carefully. In wrapping the curls, wind firmly but DO NOT pull. It is not the stretching of the hair that makes the curl. Another firm DO NOT is, avoid fish hooking the ends by rolling the hair on the rods and crimping the ends under as you roll. Always begin wrapping on the papers that are wrapped around the end of the hair. The papers should be pulled out halfway beyond the end of the hair. The rolling begins here on the paper.

Follow the timing instructions very carefully and you should achieve what you want in the curl. Most directions are fairly clear about the wave pattern, so go to it if you want to trade perms with a friend.

CARE OF THE HAIR

Unless you are one of those lucky ones who can afford to go to the salon regularly to have your hair done, you will be doing your own at home.

Having a routine is always helpful. It gives you a pattern of action. If you know you are going to wash your hair on Saturday and Wednesday nights, then you plan ahead for that and give yourself time. If you don't plan for it you will find that more often than not, something comes up that is more important or interesting to do, and there you are with less than pretty hair for a few more days.

Some of you probably have short blowdry cuts that require frequent washing. Others will have a more set style that you will

103

expect to last all week long and only wash once a week.

IS IT HARMFUL TO WASH YOUR HAIR OFTEN?

That is a good question and one I hear quite often. It depends of course on the condition of your scalp and hair. Frequent washing can dry out your hair and skin on the scalp. If you have very dry skin and hair, you will want to plan a style that is not dependent on frequent washings. If your hair is very oily you will want one that will allow you to wash frequently.

WHAT KIND OF SHAMPOOS SHOULD YOU USE?

Here again it depends a great deal on the condition of the hair. Very dry hair will benefit from an oil base shampoo which leaves a little residue of oil even after rinsing.

Very oily hair needs a shampoo that will strip the hair shaft of all excess oil. There are many, many, brand name shampoos. Just check the ingredients to be sure of what the product will do for you.

Most of our modern day shampoos are detergent based or very removable with water. You should be aware of some types of shampoo that are still around that are very good if you have very soft water to wash your hair in.

Grandmother used to save rainwater in a barrel to wash her hair in. She needed to. The soap she used was from her homemade bar soap melted down into a liquid or the bar itself. Pure castile soaps or coconut oil shampoos will only rinse out well with soft water. Soap will leave a film on your hair that sticks to those scales on the shaft of the hair. It makes the hair dull.

Another trick that Grandmother used was rinsing her hair with a tablespoon of vinegar (for dark hair) or a tablespoon of lemon juice (for light) in a cup of water. This cut the soap off the hair shaft and with lots of rinsing gave her lovely manageable hair. This is still a very useful hair rinse today to get your hair squeeky clean. Be sure to rinse and rinse until the odor is gone or you will smell like a pickle for a while.

Detergent shampoos are a little harder on the hair than soap, but well worth using for their rinsable qualities. We can add back onto the hair shaft a cream rinse or conditioner that will restore the PH balance that everyone talks about.

Most shampoos are somewhat alkaline. This substance will make the hair shaft swell and flake off. After long use even normal hair will look dull and feel stiff or like straw. An acid balanced or PH shampoo can shrink the cuticle and make the hair shaft stronger with more luster.

It is good to look for a shampoo of this type. You will find the PH balance in several types of shampoos, both liquid, paste or gels.

SHAMPOOS WITH ADDITIVES

If you are looking for a cleansing shampoo that will give special treatments to the hair, then you want one with an additive. There are many kinds of them, but the most common are egg, lemon, herbs, balsam and protein. I will discuss each of them.

Eggs

Nature lovers golden gem, the egg, has long been known for its cosmetic uses. Actually the most useful ingredient is the oil in the yolk itself. The albumin in the egg white is often dried and put in facial masques to dry on the skin for a toning treatment. The egg white dries and pulls the skin taut.

Rather than pay the extra price of egg in a shampoo, which has really very little action on the hair shaft, why not separate the yolk and apply after shampooing, allowing it to stay on the hair for about ten minutes and then rinse off with tepid water.

I will never forget my first egg treatment shampoo. I was just new in beauty college and we had learned about some of the home concoctions we could whip up in the kitchen. I shampooed my sister's hair and put a whipped egg on her head and massaged it in well. We let it stay on the hair for the prescribed ten minutes and then rinsed it out with very hot water (rather than tepid). We had scrambled egg in her hair which was really hard to rinse out. My two mistakes of course were to first, leave the whites in the egg, and

105

second, to use too hot a temperature in the water. So remember to use tepid water if you try this home treatment.

Eggs in shampoo really do rather little to help the hair because it is in the soap and will be washed off the hair shaft.

Lemon as an Additive

This is a very effective ingredient if used on especially oily hair. It has the ability to remove excess oil from the hair and scalp without making the hair brittle, dry and stiff. If your hair is dry, then lemon is not what you want because it may worsen the condition.

Herbs

There are some shampoos that use herbs effectively. Others are a gimmick to get you to buy. Established companies understand the uses of the herbs they use and you will probably get good results from the product. If you want to do your own treatment with herbs, ask the proprietor of your local herb store what to use. These people understand the many varied kinds of herbs and can tell you how to use them on the hair.

If you are a person who is bothered with allergies you might want to be a little careful with herbal concoctions.

Balsam

This is a very sticky thick substance which is taken from the bark of trees grown in the tropics. It forms a coating on the hair shaft. It will add thickness and strength to the hair.

For a while you will love the way your hair feels until it gets a build up of too much. This brings us to protein. . .

Protein, the Hair Strengthener

This too forms a coating on the hair. Do you remember that the surface of the hair has scales that lay over each other like shingles? Protein builders leave particles on the hair shaft that work into the layers of the scales on the hair. Like balsam, at first you will like the extra body and strength your hair has.

After several weeks washing with these conditioners, you begin to get a build up on the hair and you will notice that you can't do anything with it. With balsam, the hair gets very dull. With protein the scales of the hair shaft become filled with protein and the hair is coated with a brittle substance. The hair seems coarse and very dry. It will not curl as well and it is very frustrating because you keep pouring on special conditioners to correct the situation. You are just adding to the problem.

If you are going to use these conditioners, once in a while, you have to use a strong shampoo to cut the gunk off the hair shaft. I usually get out the dish drops or dish soap detergent and wash my hair with this, two full soapings. This is my miracle cure for the buildup blues.

Usually you can go one month using a conditioner of balsam or protein type and then wash with the harsher detergent every fifth time. This should keep your hair in nice condition.

AFTER CONDITIONERS

All of the before mentioned ingredients, that are sometimes used in shampoos, are really more effective and do a better job if they are used in a rinse after shampooing. They should be left on for the prescribed time, and rinsed out according to instructions. Two other kinds are solutions that are made up of either laquers, shellac or thick creams.

Shellac body builders do the most for thin very limp hair, but will tend to make it dry and bushier. Oily hair will not benefit from this treatment.

Cream rinses are created to restore the water balance of the hair. They are especially good for dry, bushy hair. Normal to oily hair will seem limp and dull.

It is a good idea to know your hair type and the kind of shampoo that will do the most for you and the conditioner you do or don't need.

HOW TO SHAMPOO

One of the best parts of going to the beauty salon is the brisk the prescribed time.

11.   Rinse out the conditioner with warm water.

12.   Gently blot the hair with a towel. It is in fragile condition at this point so do not rub too briskly.

13.   Gentle comb out and set or blowdry.

GETTING DOWN TO STYLING

There are several methods of styling the hair. You need to choose the one that works best for you and the one you, yourself can do best if you have to do your own hair.

Setting on Rollers

Tighter styles can be done when using the roller method. The hair isn't as natural looking but it will stay in for sometimes a week.

When you set your hair absolutely wet, it will dry into a firmer set. It takes longer to dry, but if you have very limp, fine hair, this may be the best method for you. You might even want to use a little setting gel to help stiffen the hair for a more lasting curl.

I know some very young girls who wash their hair and let it dry thoroughly and then set their hair on large rubber foam curlers every night. The result is softly curling hair that seems more natural. This is certainly preferable to the old rag curlers my mother used when I was a little girl. We have come a long way in our equipment and devices to make our hair more beautiful.

Pincurling

This method of hairstyling has practically gone out, but who knows, it might become fashionable again to have very tight curls and waves. Our new perms for curly styles have replaced this old method of styling, but let me describe it for you. Place the tip of the finger next to the scalp, wind hair around it and put it off the finger fastening it to the head with a bobby pin or clippie. Stand-up pin curls can be formed and then held in place with clippies. This produces a little looser curl.

shampoo that is given. Girls are trained to give a good wash and treatment to your hair. If your cosmetologist isn't giving you a good service here, then tell her exactly what you want. You are paying a good price for a shampoo set and sometimes the preliminary steps are rushed over in her attempt to get to another customer. If I wanted to do a rush shampoo, I could just as well do it at home over the kitchen sink.

This is the way I was trained to give a super shampoo and you can follow it for your home treatment as well.

A SALON SHAMPOO AT HOME

1. Comb out hair carefully, removing tangles from the ends proceeding upwards to the scalp. (Never put the comb in at the scalp and pull out to the ends until all tangles have been removed.)

2. Part the hair on the scalp with a fine-toothed comb gently scrape loose any dandruff and dirt that is stuck on the scalp. Proceed over the entire head.

3. With a firm but gentle hairbrush, brush the dandruff flakes out of the hair and carry the oil from the scalp out onto the hair shaft.

4. Massage the scalp with fingertips using a firm pressure and not sliding the fingers over the hair but trying to move the skin of the scalp. (Loose scalp is better for hair growth. A tight skin in this area sometimes leads to early baldness.)

5. Using tepid water, saturate the entire head of hair with water. Run the water slowly so as not to tangle the hair.

6. Apply a small amount of shampoo. The tendency is to add more and more to work up a lather, but the first shampooing will cut the oil of the hair. Do not waste shampoo getting a lather on the first wash.

7. Rinse hair with tepid water to remove soap.

8. Apply another small amount of shampoo. Rub the scalp briskly with the finger tips (not your fingernails). Massage and scrub all over the head to get all of the oil and soil.

9. Rinse well with tepid water and rinse more and more until hair sounds squeaky when you pull on it with the fingers.

10. Use a conditioner if wanted and let it stay on the hair for

After hair has dried, brush the hair all over into soft curls, waves, etc..

Curling Iron

After the hair has dried thoroughly from your shampoo, curl the hair with the iron all over your head by parting off sections. Roll in the directions you want the final comb-out to go. If your hair is short, you may want to do some blow drying at first because it is slow and tedious to curl the entire head of hair with the iron. Often times the curling iron lends a finishing touch to a blow dry style.

Styling with the curling iron will have to be done daily for touch-ups. When my mother was a girl, she used to get her hair marceled (set in waves) with a curling iron. The rod of the iron was much smaller in dimension and the iron was used very hot. With a comb, the hair was pushed into a wave position and crimped. When the entire head of hair was completed, it fell in waves close to the head. These hairstyles were costly for their day but the girls wore them for at least two weeks before washing and they really stayed in.

We often laugh at the old fashioned hair styles of yesteryear, but don't laugh too loudly, they can return and become an updated fashion of our day.

Blowdrying

The blowdrying is a very useful tool for getting your hair dry fast and for setting it if you can master the contraption. I have watched the girls in the salon working and working to achieve a hairstyle with blowdrying. These sets are usually more expensive than a shampoo set. No wonder! It takes so long and so much attention from the stylist. If hair is very short it might not take so long, but it really is an art in itself. I admire anyone who can do it on themselves.

Not only do you need a blowdryer, you also need a completely round brush made out of wood and hog bristles. I completely melted a plastic brush attempting to style my hair with the hot air of

110

the dryer.

If you blowdry your hair, you really need to condition it and take care of it because not only are you applying an abnormal amount of heat to the hair, you are also brushing constantly.

Electric curlers

I much prefer the electric curlers that come in a box. They fit over rods that are heated by electricity and get very hot. Either you pour water into the curler container or push them on a little squirt contraption to get moisture on the rod. They can be used without the water, but I find they are tighter with water and more lasting.

The rollers are used just like other rollers, but you can take them out after five to seven minutes or so. The hair setting is soft and natural looking and the next day you may only have to place a curl or two where your hair has gone limp.

HAIRCUTTING — THE FOUNDATION OF STYLE

We will soon talk about what kind of style you should choose for your own personal Season and shape of face, etc., but first we need to understand that the proper haircut will make or break a good set.

If you want to save money in any area, don't let it be in your haircut. Find a stylist that really knows how to cut hair well. Maybe you have a friend like I do who trades haircuts with me. We both know how we like our hair done and it is nice to be able to get a trim a little more often and it saves both of us money.

I am amused sometimes at how people pick out their beautician. They choose the one who has the nicest haircut or prettiest hair. I say, "Choose the girl or fellow who has done the work on that girl's hair."

Hair is still cut with much the same equipment as when grandmother was a girl. Scissors and razor cutting. Hair can be cut wet or dry depending on the tool used and the way your beautician was trained. I was trained to cut the hair with scissors and can slither or blunt cut the hair. The slithering method is similar to the effect

111

achieved by a razor. The razor can be used to blunt cut the hair as a scissors would. So, I feel the way your hair turns out after a cut is dependent on the skill of the operator.

If you find a good way to cut your hair, then try to stay with it.

If you have an unusual growth pattern of hair, you are going to have to style around it. Cowlicks can be an asset if you learn how to style around them. Sometimes a permanent wave will break the cowlick pattern enough to help you in combing the hair in a different direction.

STYLING YOUR HAIR TO PROPORTION

Before we go into the hair styles appropriate for the Seasons, we need to talk about what is right for YOU.

Hair is not styled just to fit your face, it should also be styled to fit your body. You must take into account every feature on your face and your body size. Consider these when styling your hair.

1. Type of hair — limp, full-bodied, long, short
2. Your height and weight — any unusual buldges
3. Shape of face looking straight into the mirror
4. Side view of nose, chin and forehead
5. Neck — long or short, thick or thin
6. Back of head — straight up and down, protruding crown

When your hair is styled, take a good look at yourself in a mirror and then back up and look into a small mirror to see the back and sides of your head. The picture has to be pleasing from all angles or it is not a good style for you.

Consider your body proportions. If you are small and pixie-like, a huge bouffant hairstyle will make you look like a mushroom. If you are heavily overweight, a huge bouffant style will accent the size as it repeats itself down below. Both persons would do well to keep hair styled more closely and softly to the head.

If you are not sure what I am talking about, have someone take a picture of you when your hair is fixed in what you consider your best style. Take a front view, full picture; a side view, both sides; and a full back view. In studying or analyzing these pictures, note how the hair either blends in with your figure or accents a bad feature.

112

This body proportion check is more important, I feel, than so much the face shape.

The face diagrams will help you find your shape of face and corrective hairstyles. Actually what you will be doing is filling in with hair in thin areas and making the hair lie flat in areas that are too wide. To add height, you wear the hair fuller on top. Look at the diagrams and study your face in the mirror. You may be a combination of two of them. If so, just consider the area where you are square and follow that correction and where you are long, etc., use another.

FACIAL CONTOURING WITH HAIR STYLES

The ideal face is divided into three parts. Using these illustrations, measure your face and decide which you are most like.

1. The narrowest part of my face is _____
2. The widest part of my face is _____
3. The shape of my face is most like the _____ diagram.

OVAL

DON'T   DO

Don't cover all of your forehead with bangs.
Do retain the oval shape with your hairline.

113

ROUND

DON'T   DO

This face should be lengthened.

The coiffure should, therefore, have more height than width.

Don't slick it back where it can't help detract from roundness.

Do lengthen your face by having a built-up hair style above the ears.

Do use a side rather than a middle part.

Do build your hair higher on one side than on the other.

HEART-SHAPED

DON'T   DO

Coiffures that are widest below the temple line are best for the heart-shaped face.

114

Don't build additional width at the temples.

Do cover some of the wide expanse of the forehead with bangs.

Do use softness.

DIAMOND

DON'T   **DO**

Hairstyle should broaden the forehead and the narrow chin line.

Don't add length to your face by having your hair too short or too long.

Do wear a bang. **Do** wear your hair wide across the jaw to fill in and give bulk to your narrow chin.

SQUARE

DON'T   **DO**

Variety in line and not too much bang on the forehead are best.

Don't accent the squareness with a hairstyle that repeats this line.

Do counteract the squareness with a hairstyle that has an uneven silhouette.

OBLONG

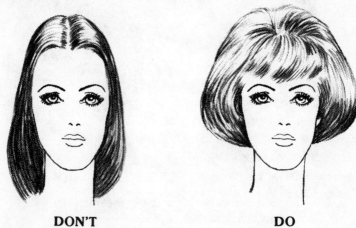

DON'T   DO

The hairstyle that is widest in the middle of the head is best for this face.

Don't emphasize the long line with hanging hair.

Do balance the face with an asymmetrical bang.

STYLING FOR THE SEASONS

If you will promise to look at yourself as an individual and wear your hair in an attractive style suited to your own personality and body pattern, I will give you some general rules for hairstyles that will be good for your Season's fashion look.

These hints are for you to try, and if they don't work exactly for you, then perhaps you can incorporate a part of them to achieve what is best for you.

Telling all Winter persons to wear their hair up in a little knot on the head, because simplicity is so becoming to a Winter, is rather like telling a bald man to brush his hair into a windblown style.

116

You might be a Winter, like me, who has a ski-jump nose. From the side, that kind of style is very unbecoming to me. I have a Winter friend, however, that looks absolutely gorgeous with her hair pulled back and pulled into a french knot. It is my very favorite of the several ways she can wear her hair.

You will just have to experiment with some of these hints for your Season until you find something perfect for yourself.

SUMMER HAIR STYLING

The summer look is soft and feminine. Hair is best when it waves or curls softly around the face. It may be long or short, but the curls should not be the tight, springy type that Springs wear so well. Hair may be pulled up into soft curls at the crown with tendrils pulled out and curled hanging in front of the ear and at the nape of the neck. Severe lines should be avoided as it might make your conservative coloring seem stern. If hair is coarse, either curl it, or blowdry in soft waves rather than sleek blunt cuts.

Little ribbons and bows and flowers in the hair give a Summer femininity.

Copy Grace Kelly and Cheryl Teigs who are Summer in appearance.

117

SPRING HAIRSTYLES

Bouncy curls all over the head are good for Spring, as is longer hair feathered back or in poofy bangs and curls on the end. Soft and natural is the look for Spring. Hair may be cut in little boy short cuts that pixie around the face or permanented in a curly-do. Hair should have a shine and a bounce when you walk. Braids and ribbons and bows tied on the end for casual fun.

Copy Suzanne Somers, Lucille Ball, Doris Day, Carol Burnett, and Dinah Shore.

AUTUMN HAIRSTYLES

Business-like and sophisticatedly simple, this is Autumn's look. Long hair is better in controlled styles. Page boys, sleek and simple, easy to care for all speak Autumn. Strive for a metallic sheen and sharp angles rather than curls. If hair is short and styled in curls, keep it simple and not bouffant and dressey. No curly tendrils or fluffy styles. Hair may be worn long and straight or with a slight bounce or curl, but not too fussy.

Copy Katherine Hepburn, Kate Jackson, Susan Hayward, Jane Fonda, all Autumn stars.

WINTER HAIRSTYLES

A dramatic style is best for you, depending on the degree of contrast you have in your body design. Softly curled or waved hair is good on a round faced Winter. Curly afros are only good on black Winters. Here again there is always an exception. At one of my classes I color-coded a lovely Winter person whose hair was curled into a short afro. Taking into account that she had such fine, limp

120

hair, and very little of it, this style was best for her, even though it was not classically Winter.

Long hair styled in various dramatic ways, hanging loosely, over one eye effect, parted in the middle, pulled back and fastened in the back, fastened up into a French knot, braided and wrapped around the head, are good.

Short hair should not be severely styled as this is a business woman's style. Get a winged back effect or soft simple bang across the forehead with large waves or curls.

Copy Elizabeth Taylor or Cher or Suzanne Pleshett. They are all Winters.

Be ready for the compliments you will receive when you dress in right colors in your own personal style and set it all off with lovely cosmetic colors and crowned with a perfect hairstyle for you and your Season.

122

COLOR: ITS EFFECT ON YOU
AND OTHERS

In the original text of **Color Me A Season,** I covered the subject of How To Find and Use Your Most Flattering Colors. The main context of that work concerned you and your personal color design.

In preparing for that first writing venture, I found many books on color theory and art, but none pertaining to the coloring of human beings. There are a few written on the psychology of color and its effect on people. One missing factor is present in these works that I feel is important enough to bring to you, that of the four Seasons' color pallets, or bouquets as I sometimes call them, and their effect on us.

It is not enough to say that red is a passionate color. Taking Spring's red, we find a psychological effect of brightness and cheeriness. We think of Christmas and high school cheerleaders. It is a color that *moves* us and our emotions.

Winter's red, in contrast, gives a sultry, more romantic feeling. We think of Spanish ladies with their mantillas and a red rose clenched in their teeth, of bing cherries lusciously waiting to be plucked from the tree.

You already know, if you are a Spring cheerleader type, you should stick to the red that most fits you, etc. I will not go into much actual material that was already covered in the original text, but more into the theory of color, taking it from a standpoint of the differences between the four Season's colors.

Most of us never realize how color is used by the business world to affect us. We purchase certain products because the colors on the labels move us to buy them. We attend restaurants that have the right atmosphere (color). We never realize that we are being shuffled in and out of fast food places because the colors

123

come from the contrasting yellow and blue under-based tones. They give us a feeling of uneasiness so that we don't linger in the establishment to talk and visit, but make room for more people.

There are just all kinds of ways that color can be used to benefit us if we know how to go about it. Let's get into it. . .

As we discuss color, I think you will find it useful to have a means of communicating about it.

You might find it helpful to get out the box of 64 Crayola®. Crayons that you used for finding your Season or open the book, **Color Me A Season,** to back color wheel diagram and color bouquets.

If you have the profesional **Color Me A Season** color fan for the four Seasons, you will find that useful, too.

Another good color communicator is a Grumbacher® Color Computer which you can purchase in most artist supply stores.

THE COLOR WHEEL
Primary Colors

There are really only three colors of the color wheel that stand as actual, original color. No other color was used to make them. They stand alone and are the first of Primary colors. Every other color is made from these hues.

Red is considered a warm color.

Yellow is also a warm hue.

Blue is a cool tone.

The Primaries are stark and bold. Winter people have these in their color bouquet. These three colors make the boldest color statement because they are pure in tone. They provide a lot of contrast in a color scheme and will take the attention away from any other color you put with them.

When all three are put together in like areas they vie for attention and it makes us feel uneasy. Even two together are too intense to be comfortable.

One popular toy company manufactures many of their toys for tots under three in red, yellow and blue color schemes. They are bright and cheerful and keep a child busy manipulating and working with the toy which they would be less likely to do if it were

124

all one solid color.

Secondary Colors

By mixing our three Primary hues, we come up with some more colors for our wheel. Blue and yellow make green, red and yellow make orange, and red and blue make purple. We now have a color wheel of six colors instead of three.

Orange is considered a warm tone and green is cool, but on the warm side also. Purple is the coolest of all and is the one color that reaches us from the sun's spectrum last. That is why we think of faraway mountains as purple in a picture.

Anytime you wear purple it will make you appear to be smaller because it recedes back away from the eye.

Tertiary Colors

The Tertiaries are the mixes of the basic six on the wheel. Red-orange, yellow-orange, yellow-green, blue-green, blue-violet, and red-violet.

In my color studio I have a paint display rack that features 1001 colors. All of these are simply mixes of the twelve colors on the color wheel. Some are very intense (bright) and others are light tints (white added).

Some of the colors are dull or muted. This is achieved by taking the color directly across the color wheel (the Complimentary shade) and mixing a little of it in with the main color, such as yellow-green. We come up with a color like olive-green. Many of Autumn's colors are mixed in this way.

A NEW NEED FOR COLOR KNOWLEDGE

Our pilgrim fathers had little need to be color analyzed or to learn how to use color to please themselves and others. They had very little color to use. Their clothing was basically in blacks, white, grays and perhaps a little blue or red when naturally grown roots and plants could be used to provide a dye. These at best were very poor, considering the modern methods we have today to put color into our lives.

Today we have a myriad of color hues all around us to pick and choose from. It becomes confusing and mind boggling just to decorate a room in our homes, or put together a well coordinated outfit of clothing.

Getting your colors into four areas will be extremely beneficial to you in realizing the effect the four Seasons' colors will have when you use them.

As a color analyst I have a definite advantage to determine how people are affected by color.

Although Luscher's *Color Test* (a very popular book which contains a color test to determine your personality) has sold in the millions, I feel it would add to the dimension of the color testing to realize that the four Seasons' personalities will respond to the eight colors used in a much different way.

Johannes Itten's subjective colors are much more accurate in finding personality. Psychologically we are influenced by our Season when it comes to color. While Spring individuals enjoy yellow, Winters are afraid to wear it. Before I drape the yellow for Winter bouquet from my color rod, I can anticipate the reaction from a truly Winter person. Most of them will say, "I like that shade of yellow but I would never choose to wear it."

As a Winter myself, I understand completely how they feel. In my entire life I have only had one yellow dress, and though I could see that it seemed to be an attractive color on me, I was so uncomfortable while wearing it that it saw its way recently to the Goodwill.

When I choose yellow again, it will be in a blouse to be worn with a black or white suit, or in little bits of color in a print or scarf. My personality just can't handle it when I wear it.

On the other hand, you should see the wall in my living room — Winter yellow. It cheers me up to be in that room, but I don't want to wear it. The outside of our house this year is getting a new coat of paint . . . bright yellow, with a Winter dark brown trim. I am using yellow, you see, but surrounding it with a safe, dark, hiding color. It shows so much my Winter-Spring personality

126

blend.

Yellow, then, has an entirely different connotation to each personality. It appears to me to be quite evident that if a subjective color test is given, we can find our predominate Season's traits and also our blending personality of one or two other Seasons. The amazing fact is that we also find those same designs in the pattern of the iris of the eye.

Let me discuss a few case histories from a subjective color test that I have devised and use at the studio before each color analysis.

TESTING FOR SUBJECTIVE COLORS

Before I proceed with a color analysis, whether with a group or with an individual, I do a test of subjective colors. This is mostly for research and my use to see how much a person recognizes his/her own colors.

It is entirely necessary that the person being tested be completely devoid of any color information about the four pallets. I find that if the individual being tested has any previous knowledge about color division, they are influenced to some extent as to their favorite (or subjective) colors.

Some persons have decided before they come to be analyzed that they would like to be a certain Season. Sometimes this happens to be the very one they actually are, but sometimes not.

I am careful not to display posters or any visual aids that will give them previous feelings about the four color pallets.

I have eight cards upon which the four Season's shades or tints of a particular color on the color wheel are represented as follows:

Card 1 RED	**Card 2 BLUE**
Summer blue-red	Summer pastel blue
Winter dark, pure red	Winter pure blue
Spring bright red	Spring royal blue
Autumn red-orange	Autumn blue-green

127

Card 3   YELLOW
Summer pastel yellow
Winter medium yellow
Spring bright yellow
Autumn yellow-gold

Card 4   ORANGE
Summer pastel peach
Winter salmon pink
(dark)
Spring melon (an
orange-pink)
Autumn orange

Card 5   GREEN
Summer pastel mint
green
Winter very dark green
Spring bright kelly green
with yellow added
Autumn olive green

Card 6   PURPLE
Summer light lavender
Winter red-violet
Spring light blue-violet
Autumn pure violet

Card 7   BROWN
Summer light grey-
brown
Winter dark chocolate
brown
Spring yellow-brown
Autumn pure brown
(warm)

Card 8   TURQUOISE
(universal color)
Summer very pale tur-
quoise
Winter very dark tur-
quoise
Spring medium turquoise
Autumn green turquoise

By crayon name, as listed in **Color Me A Season** for the color bouquets, they are as follows:

Summer	Winter	Spring	Autumn
magenta	maroon	red (with some red-orange yellow over)	
sky blue	blue	cornflower	blue-green
lemon yellow peach	yellow (med.) salmon	yellow (bright) melon	goldenrod orange
sea green	pine green	yellow-green (dark)	olive green

128

| lavender | red-violet | periwinkle | violet |

| raw umber (lt.) | | raw sienna | |
| | raw umber (drk) | | burnt sienna |

| turquoise blue (light) | turquoise blue (dark) | turquoise blue | blue-green |

These cards are handed one at a time to the person being tested. Time is allowed for contemplation, but if there is any reluctance to choose a color, I ask them why they are having a difficult time. I assure them that no one can ever fail a color test and to choose the color they most like, one that is a real favorite, with no thought of how it is used.

Some are influenced by their size or environmental influences to such a degree that they have a very difficult time choosing color. When they really let themselves choose favorite colors, they find they can hardly relax while doing so.

I find most individuals take a little longer to make their decision on each card, but in a group situation there are those who choose what someone else does, especially those individuals who have a hard time making up their minds.

The two most rejected color cards are, first, purple, and then yellow. I do not know if there is any connection, but find it interesting that these two are compliments on the color wheel.

Most everyone enjoys the blue colors with red holding a close second. Green and brown are tied in third position with orange and turquoise coming in fourth.

In the case of rejected purple, I think it may be because so much superstition is involved with the color and the fact that it has in the past been a royal color, not given to the ranks of common people. People are afraid to wear it. Yellow is so bright and intense that most feel they will shine like the color does. Usually upon questioning, I find these individuals fond of yellow as an accent or paint color in their room.

Children test more purely for their subjective colors. Men are more conservative with color, but in their testing they like blue and red cards equally and dislike, more than women, the brown. Most have been so influenced into an understated color pallet because of their sex, that it is hard for them to choose the brighter colors on the color cards. They pick the lighter colors, generally, or those that do not come on too strong (red being the exception).

GENERAL FINDINGS FOR THE SEASONS

Choosing the most reflective of the testings that I have done, I will report on three individuals for each Season. Many more tests have been given, but to keep up your interest, here they are as follows.

SUMMER PERSONS BEING TESTED

Summer Number 1: This individual was a woman who appeared to be very conservative. She was reluctant to wear very much cosmetic color after the analysis for Summer even though the colors of the Summer makeup are very conservative in themselves.

Of the eight colors, five choices were made from the Summer bouquet colors. She chose two Winter colors, but she chose from the cool side of the color wheel blue and purple (red-violet). She also showed a marked preference for the purple colors and had a hard time choosing between Summer or Winter purple.

Inasmuch as Summer and Winter are corresponding color bouquets on the more quiet side of the color spectrum, it still showed her to be conservative in personality. Spring brown (yellow-brown) and melon (darker pinkish orange) were preferred on the brown and orange cards.

She came up six points for the Summer-Winter quiet side and two points for the Spring-Autumn.

Eye pattern: The design in the iris of the eye was very crackled, like a purely Summer design. Some Spring sunburst was present.

Skin tone: Complexion was very pale with a slight yellow tinge but blue undertone. The yellow in skin tone led her to

130

believe that gold jewelry was better on her, but she could readily see that silver was better for her.

Personality type: This was a more absolute Summer with some Spring in personality. Quite set in her ways, this individual would benefit from enlarging on the Spring openness in her personality blend.

If Summer persons are not careful, they can become quite stubborn and unmoveable in their old age.

Summer Number 2: This individual was a man whose color choices numbered seven Summer and one Winter. One Spring color was chosen, but as an alternate to Summer light peach.

This individual broke the rule on liking red because he was thinking of himself wearing the color. He confessed that he would like to have his wife wear it and also the brighter Winter yellow.

His favorite color choices were blue and gray (typical of a Summer individual).

Eye pattern: Design in the iris showed two possible markings with the Summer cracked glass taking precedence over the other one. A few Autumn specks were present.

Skin tone: Very light, though darker than a Summer woman's would be. Ruddiness to the nose and cheeks, but not predominate. Much blue showing in the underlying skin.

Personality: Again, a conservative individual, but with stronger convictions. Not liable to speak up, but when angered, very strong and assertive. Extremely set in his ways. More energetic than most Summer individuals. I feel the personality type of this man would be termed Summer-Autumn, with the highest percentage falling into the Summer characteristic area.

Summer Number 3: In a group of Girl Scouts, I found this delightful Summer girl who was ten years of age. She was the only Summer found that night in a group of fourteen girls.

While teaching the girls about color, this girl caught my eye because she was more quiet and less talkative than the rest, and had a shyness about her, yet much poise.

Her color choices numbered three Summer, two Winter, two Springs and no Autumn. (She failed to make one choice as the cards numbered eight.) In revealing all the four Season's color bouquets that I have represented on four large posters, I asked the girls to choose which group of entire colors they would pick as a favorite set of colors. This Summer chose the Winter colors over the Summer ones. (See her eye pattern for an interesting comparison.)

Her color choices revealed a person who fairly well knew her conservative nature with a little bit of the Winter poise and outgoingness of Spring.

Eye pattern: Very Summer cracked glass with some evidence of Spring and a possible Winter spoke.

Skin tone: Very light with light ash blond hair.

Personality type: Summer-Winter, more percentage falling to the Summer side. The third less blend of Spring gave a warmness to the personality. On her paper during the color testing she doodled a cute train engine (some Spring showing up).

WINTER PERSONALITY COLOR TESTING

Winter Number 1: Female. Color choices numbered five Winter, no Summer, one Spring and two Autumn. This woman was very hard to analyze just from looking at her own color design. Her medium brown hair seemed to have an Autumn or Spring cast and the skin was freckled. One would not think of her as a contrasting Winter. Color testing proved the seemingly impossible true, and all Winter colors were better on her.

Personality of this individual was friendly and warm, but she admittedly was quite happy just being with her own family. She was also prone to be a little aloof and uninterested in others outside her own inner circle of friends and relatives.

Proper Winter cosmetics made a tremendous difference on her, and she was so much improved by them that it was quite breathtaking to see the before and after of this color transformation.

Eye pattern: Spring's sun surrounding an Autumn pattern which connected itself to the pupil. Faint Winter spoke design also present.

Complexion type: Blue undertoned requiring a Winter color

132

foundation. The freckles were inherited, undoubtedly, from an Autumn or Spring mother or father, but the surrounding skin tone called for Winter Rose Blush foundation.

Personality type: Winter-Spring. She was very quiet and agreeable during our color testing and analysis and quite cooperative in changing over to Winter's colors from the Spring ones previously chosen to wear because of her hair and freckled skin.

Winter Number 2: This gentleman could certainly be classed purely on the Summer-Winter side. All color choices fell into those two Seasons. He had a particular liking for blue and was very conservative with color.

Eye pattern: Brown eyes with spoke design present present coming from a brown design around the pupil of the eye.

Complexion type: Very light, almost as light as Summer Number 2, but with more of a porcelain quality, less transluscent and no particular blueness coming through, more of a gray tone to the skin. (Winters rarely have a healthy pink tone.)

Personality type: Winter-Summer* in personality, this man was very poised and quiet spoken. During the class he did his share of adding to information being shared. Quite knowledgeable, he showed his Winter nature in wanting to be the center of attention while at the same time trying to remain humble about it.

Winter Number 3: Female. This olive skin toned individual felt that she should choose gold metals and warm colors. She had preconceived ideas about color before testing, but chose Four Winter out of eight test colors. One Summer Color (light blue), and two Autumn colors were chosen (purple and warm brown). Spring melon was also chosen.

Eye pattern: Brown eyes with many spokes with one or two Autumn specks.

Complexion type: Olive tones, but with a blue or gray undertone. Very dark hair. This was truly a very contrasting Winter and improved her appearance a great deal with Winter colors. The Autumn tones she had been wearing turned her olive complexion into orange instead of the bronze effect of Autumn.

Personality type: Winter-Autumn. A strong-headed person who was opinionated, but willing to accept other opinions. She readily saw the differences in the color draping of the Winter colors compared to the other four Seasons' tones. This woman showed dramatic leadership qualities.

SPRING PERSONALITY COLOR TESTING

Spring Number 1: This young girl of six chose a varied color pallet, but it was my opinion that the child was fond of color of all kinds. She had an artistic talent that was showing up at a very young age and had been given the opportunity to use crayons and paints as much as she liked. She seemed to prefer the Spring colors, but also the pure red, yellow and blue of the Winter pallet.

Eye pattern: A pure Spring sunburst surrounding the gray doughnut separating space around the pupil of the eye. Eyes were blue and there were no other apparent markings.

Complexion type: A medium, radiant yellow skin tone.

Personality type: An absolute Spring. This delightful Spring child was continually talking, jumping, and doing. She was a people-pleaser and wanted much attention and assurance. Her mother mentioned that she got along well in school and was well-liked by her teacher and had many friends.

Spring Number 2: This quiet, conservative woman came in for a personal analysis. I had seen her previously and had thought that she would be a Summer individual because of her personality traits. She was not a smiling, happy person, but pleasant. I was surprised by her statement that she often chose the warm yellows and caramels to wear to cheer herself up. At a younger age she had worn, basically, a blue color pallet, but was trying to get more warmth into her colors for herself.

Color choices revealed she was half and half in her color choices between the two color sides. Any of the colors that were warm, such as yellow, orange and red, she picked in a pastel

134

(Summer) form. She only chose two Spring colors, brown and green.

Eye pattern: There was so much of the Summer design in the eye that I felt surely this woman had to be Summer, but there was also present some partial sunburst coming from a blue pattern surrounding the pupil. Color draping showed her to be on the Spring side of the color spectrum, but in very light pastels.

These are the individuals who often get put in Summer colors because of the effect of Spring brights on the complexion.

Complexion type: Her coloring was in the mid-range and not so light, but it was still overpowered by the brighter Spring colors UNTIL she had on her correct cosmetic colors. She then looked great in the brights and pastels.

I double checked the complexion in this case because it was hard for me to believe such a serious person could be Spring. The patch test of Spring's mid-toned foundation and Summer's mid-tone showed that the Spring color blended in, while the Summer one stayed on top.

You would have been as thrilled as she and I both were when the makeup analysis was completed. The transformation to a radiant glow was all this lady needed to cheer herself up.

Personality type: After visiting for awhile, I determined that this was a Spring-Summer blend. I would have classified her into the more serious nature of Summer, but it was evident that many recent problems had caught her in a down swing of depression from which she was slowly emerging. Her Season analysis will be extremely helpful to her in changing her life to a more cheerful pattern.

Spring Number 3: This man was an outgoing teasing type of individual whose color choices showed strong tendencies to the Winter bouquet. Many spring colors were liked, but the darker colors were chosen because of fear of wearing such unconservative colors.

Here again I find that men will not let themselves go with color choice. They are afraid to choose color most times and prefer to let someone else color code the outfits they wear.

They tend to let someone else choose the paint to paint the house. They are, however, quite firm on the color of car they want to purchase.

Eye pattern: A speckled ring of gold and bronze going around the pupil separated by a lighter area. Winter spokes present. Color draping was done to determine the Season.

Complexion type: Medium yellow tones with some ruddiness to cheeks when excited.

Personality type: Spring-Winter. When Spring is mixed with Winter there is a real insecurity problem. This individual was outgoing, but very worrisome about hurting someone or feeling hurt himself. In the group, he teased but then apologized if he needed to or not. The darker colors of Winter made him feel more secure although the skin tone was more attractive in Spring's yellow-toned bouquet. He readily accepted my advice to wear the browns of his pallet since his hair was golden and to use the brighter colors in ties or sportshirts. In this way he could remain fairly neutral in color tone and not deaden his complexion with overly dark colors.

AUTUMN PERSONALITY COLOR TESTING

Autumn Number 1: Although Autumns generally know just what to wear, they sometimes are quite mixed up when it comes to the subjective color test. This female chose seven Summer colors and one Spring. I had a difficult time convincing her she was Autumn. She had made up her mind before she came that she was Summer. She was happy when the class was completed, and she could see how lovely she was in the earth toned pallet.

I always sigh with relief when completing a color class with an argumentative Autumn individual in it. In this case, the woman purchased a complete set of cosmetics and went away happy as a lark. The rest of the color class is always affected by this type of person; as they not only argue about their own colors, they throw in their opinion about the other people in their colors, too.

Eye pattern: Color choices were so conservative I tried to see evidence of Summer pattern, but not much was present. This was a blue-on-blue autumn design with many freckles and dots.

Complexion: Light and gold undertoned. The more vibrant Autumn colors did much to enhance this woman's appearance. She had been wearing her colors too light.

Personality type: Absolute Autumn. Not much blend of another Season was present to help tone down the Choloric* temperament of Autumn.

Autumn Number 2: Another girl Scout, this girl had strong leadership qualities and knew her color side very well. She chose three Autumn and three Spring colors out of the eight choices. It is not abnormal for a young Autumn individual to like some of the brighter colors of Spring. In fact, a lot of young children love bright colors.

I have one granddaughter whom we feel is Autumn, but she is so young and pretty that the Spring colors are quite nice on her too. When she reaches her more sophisticated age, she will probably be a lot better in the Autumn bouquet.

Eye pattern: Brown-eyed with an aztec sun pattern around the pupil with some gold colorings.

Complexion: Mid-tone and somewhat olive. Her skin was lovely in Autumn colors and took on a metallic cast. Hair coloring picked up in gold tones with proper colors too.

Personality: Autumn-Spring. As I said before, this girl was a self-appointed leader, and the girls seemed to recognize this ability. She listed on her sheet the names of all the girls in the troop with their Seasons. Making lists and organizing are Autumn qualities.

Enough of Spring was present in the personality, evidenced by the gold in the eye pattern, that this girl was quite likeable.

Autumn Number 3: In looking through my color testings, I tried to come up with some that indicated more of an Autumn choice, but here again I find that on paper they don't do so well,

*Hippocrates' theory of the four types of temperament. Choloric being the most disagreeable.

but in their clothing they do. Most Autumns come to color class dressed in the right colors, more so than any other season.

This individual chose six on the Summer and Winter side, mostly Summer. The only way I can explain this is that all of the colors are so pure in tone on the color test cards that Autumns, being the conservative lot they are, will choose the light pastels rather than choose something that they feel would be bright or garish. They dress mostly in browns and this individual chose both Autumn and Spring brown plus the gold off the yellow card. They generally recognize that they cannot wear either yellow or pink very well.

Eye pattern: Blue on blue aztec sun pattern, but with much Summer cracked glass which explained the conservative pastel color choices. Some Autumn flecks present also.

Complexion type: Light and metallic with gold undertone. These are the individuals who fit into the pastel Autumn category. They look better in the pastels BUT in Autumn bouquets. When correct cosmetics are applied, they have a wide choice of color in the lights and darks of the color bouquet.

Personality type: Autumn-Summer. A super conservative individual with a much more pleasant way of presenting her doubts about color. Even though this lady seemingly accepted her analysis of color and seemed pleased about her appearance, I know that she will likely have a harder time adapting to it, more so even than our absolute Autumn who argued about it so much.

As I mentioned in **Color Me A Season,** I enjoy the open frankness of an absolute Autumn person, and they are the ones who will stick to the program of color when they have received proof that it works best for them.

These color testings, though important, do not form the basis for my Season Analysis at the time they are given. They have been helpful to me at times, as I look back at them, to try to understand why the individual has chosen as he/she has, but mostly I feel they are valuable for scientific research which is bound to follow since this area of psychology has been opened up and has proven so effective in finding personality types through color and color choice.

I have adapted the following form for my subjective color test which I give my clients during a Season Analysis. It is reproduced here for your use.

Please check with the four bouquets of color in the back of **Color Me A Season** to get the proper colors to use for testing on the eight color cards.

SUBJECTIVE COLOR TEST

by Bernice Kentner

Try to clear your mind of all preconceived ideas you may already have about the colors in this test.

Choose the one color off the card that you most like and feel drawn to.

Do not let other people's opinions in the room influence your color choice. There are no right or wrong colors. All are acceptable.

See chart on page 18 . . .

MARK ONLY ONE COLOR
If you must choose another, make it second choice.

Color	Number One	Number Two	Number Three	Number Four
Red				
Blue				
Yellow				
Orange				
Green				
Purple				
Brown				
Turquoise				

Which of all the eight colors is your favorite? _____
Which is your least favorite?   _____

_____

After viewing the entire color bouquet for each of the four Seasons, which one do you like the most? _____

Which one do you like the least?_____

What is your actual Season? (to be filled out after your analysis)

_____

Line your cards up so that all the Seasons' colors will appear on the cards as follows: Number 1 color, Summer; Number 2 color, Winter; Number 3 color, Spring; Number 4 color, Autumn.

Do not mark your cards by Season's names, but have them

lined up in order so that you know that if Number 1 is chosen, it is Summer, etc.

Color Chin Board cards can be used for the subjective color tests. You can also use material cut from the pattern for the Color Drapes. Match your test colors to those Bouquet strips in front of the Color Fans.

The Chin Board Draping Cards are laminated with clear plastic and will last a long time.

It may be that the names of Seasons on the bottom of the cards should be covered over with paper taped down so the individuals being tested will not have any preconceived ideas about which colors they should choose.

Now that there are so many people aware of the Seasonal Color Schemes, they may choose the colors they have memorized from previous color books or color pallets. This, also effects the results of the test. For this reason the color Consultant should not place much emphasis on the subjective testing to discover the color pallets individuals should wear.

Color drapes of material may also be laid out for color choices on the subjective color tests. This is especially effective in a lecture before a large audience. Cloth may be held up one by one for all to see in sequence of order as laid out on the column.

HOW THE INDIVIDUAL COLORS AFFECT THE SEASON'S PERSONALITIES

My years of experience of color draping individuals to determine their Seasons has given me a terrific opportunity to observe their reactions to the colors of their own bouquet.

THE EFFECT OF COLOR ON SPRING

The most favorite color of Springs is melon (a peachy pink). It is very attractive on most every one of them. This is the color I

141

strive for in cosmetic colors — a peaches and cream look.

The second best color for Springs is usually turquoise blue. Most of them have not found it as a color, but they love it ever afterwards.

Many blue-eyed Springs try to wear blue eyeshadow. This is not a good color for them because it is too cool. We switch them to turquoise which is a little brighter because of the yellow that is in the green mixed with pure blue to obtain turquoise.

An absolute Spring person will love all of his/her colors bright. Yellow and red are especially liked.

Springs have a nonchalant attitude about their beige, carmel browns and darker yellow-brown. It is almost as if they don't exist as colors. Once the colors are pointed out to them as wonderful neutral colors to wear the brighter colors with, then they are interested in them.

When Springs are a blend with another Season's type in their personality, they will sometimes avoid their own bright colors. The interesting things is that most will not go into the neutrals of another Season, but more into the muted darker colors such as dark red, dark blue, dark green, etc.

A lot of Springs like blue and have a tendency to choose too light a tint of it. They should use the brighter blues and stay away from pastels. Color draping will show them how faded their complexion looks in Summer's light blue.

The yellow-greens are accepted by Springs, but many of them either just love them or do not like to wear them. When they will not choose this bright tone, they sometimes go into the pastel of Summer or the dark Winter, a conservative Season's blend showing up perhaps.

Periwinkle blue (a purple blue in light tones) is hardly ever chosen by a Spring. It is extremely attractive on them, but they are not apt to choose it for a clothing color. It is perhaps too cool for them, but they should try it, especially those who have blue eyes.

Springs need bright color on their body, if not in the clothing, then on the face. There needs to be a good color balance between makeup and bright colors.

The very bright clothing colors will fade out cosmetic shades, so more needs to be applied to obtain a balance.

Many Springs have gotten by for years with their own healthy glow. When it begins to fade, they are sometimes reluctant to touch up their cosmetic colors. Once they see themselves in them, they are convinced.

CONSERVATIVE SPRING'S COLOR EFFECT

If the personality blend is anything but absolute Spring, then our Springs (in color type) are going to be more conservative in color choice.

They should not wear the more muted colors, but if they just cannot bring themselves to dress so brightly, then I advise them to use some of Autumn's bouquet for skirts or slacks or use their own neutral browns from their own bouquet of colors to feel more comfortable in color. If they wear all neutrals, they must tone up their blush and lipstick or eye colors to get radiance to the skin tone or they will look all beige and uninteresting.

A Spring-Summer may mistakingly wear light colors from the Summer bouquet. If skin tone allows, they may go pastel, but in Spring's yellow-based colors instead.

A Spring-Autumn will often choose Autumn colors to wear. Though not terrible, they tend to make them look older and more tired.

A Spring-Winter will often go to the darker navy blue, red and more subdued yellows and greens of Winter. They will try to wear black and if their hair is dark, they should wear a bright Spring colored blouse with it rather than over the entire body. I cannot take it away from them if they have a feeling for it.

BLACK FOR SPRING OR AUTUMNS

There is a black that is better on Springs and Autumns. It has some yellow in it. By itself it is not a very attractive color (to me, a Winter, that is). When worn correctly, it can be very nice.

Jane Fonda is a definite Autumn individual. At this year's Academy Awards she came on stage wearing a yellow-based black dress with sequins in the front. Most of the yellow-black came close to her face. I have never seen her more beautiful, and she looked much better than in the other blacks I have seen her wear before.

For your convenience I will include some of Chapter 9 "Colors for All Occasions" from **Color Me A Season.**

There are some moments in our lives that we want to be wearing just the right color for the effect to match the occasion.

SPRING

Fun and Sun

Spring greens
Red
Pink
Bright blue
Bright yellow and gold
Off-white combined with
  above

Business

Off-white with small touches
  of bright colors
Off-white with browns

Rust
Navy blue with small touches
  of Spring colors

Solemn Occasions

Navy blue
Spring browns and off-white
Dark blue

Romance

Peach or melon
Periwinkle blue
Red
Light turquoise

SPRING'S COLOR SURROUNDINGS

Springs will feel more cheerful when wearing or surrounding themselves with brighter color hues from the Spring bouquet.

IMPORTANT NOTE

Just because your personality has a blend of another Season, you should always remember to wear the colors that match your skin tone (your Season). You might enjoy having some of your

Season's blend's colors in your home or around yourself in areas of color that do not affect your appearance.

Have you ever gotten up in the morning and put on a drab dress when you are already feeling down or depressed? The effect is not good. Try instead wearing one of your brighter colors from your bouquet to pick you up.

My own Season's blend is Winter-Spring and I could live quite happily in a Spring decor. I think I would have to have some of Winter's colors here and there to stabilize my feelings.

In the booklet *Interior Decorating for Your Season,* I go into the effects of color in your home, but suffice it to say that all of us need quiet retreats and cheerful areas around us to keep a good balance of the way we feel. We *can* achieve this with our own color bouquets or by using some from our opposite corresponding Season or our personality blend. (Caution here, though.) In decorating a home you should not go across from the gold-based colors into the blue undertones. They will fight each other and not be a happy combination.

AUTUMN'S FEELINGS ABOUT COLOR

Autumns are in love with brown. To them it is a color and not a neutral. They wear a lot of it and are very comfortable around it. I can remember an Autumn who made the remark, "Take any color away from me but brown, and I will be happy."

They often use any color of brown and are not too bad off in doing so, but the warm brown of their bouquet is much more becoming on them.

Olive green is another comfort color, but kelly green, which is also theirs, is almost too bright for them in feeling. This seems odd inasmuch as orange and red-orange are not only good colors for them, but ones they readily wear. If you want to hear complaints, just bring yellow near, or pink. Now pink I will agree with, but yellow, when it is in the form of gold, is very becoming.

A lot of Autumns have red or brown hair, and gold is very complimentary to that and the brown eyes that often go with the Season.

The pure violet from the color wheel scares Autumns until they see how beautiful it is on them. Those Autumns with grey hair are especially attractive in it.

Here again, I am prejudiced because I love the entire purple card of all four Season's hues. I once had a purple dress that I unwillingly gave up after finding out that it wasn't as becoming as it was just a favorite color for me.

When you put pure purple on anyone, it brings up the yellow in the complexion. On an Autumn person the effect is very nice, as the skin tone falls in the gold area anyway and it adds to a metallic cast.

Conservative Autumns love blue. In the beginning of my color analysis training I was taught that they could not wear either Navy or light blue, only turquoise. I had so many Autumns argue with me about the light blue they could wear that I put on a search for the color they were talking about. I found it! A lovely light steel blue, or yellow-based blue.

This only fortifies my findings that all of us can wear any color as long as we get enough of the underbase color ingredient in it that makes it right for us.

Navy blue is a color that is appreciated by Autumn, and they recognize that unless their hair is very colorful they had best wear a little brighter color with it.

Some want to wear black, but most of them should not unless they can get that yellowed black that I was talking about earlier. Most are willing to stick to their browns and caramels and rusts as neutral tones.

The color bouquet does not include gray, but there is one that is good. This is again a yellow-based gray and one should search the degree of darkness or lightness That is most becoming. The color fans have a strip of gray in them for each Season for finding the right one for a neutral choice as long as it is worn with a very bright color.

Autumns use color well for themselves and surround themselves with it in their homes. They try to force their colors on other people. For instance, they dislike pink so much they try to talk others out of it. Their own pink is a melon or apricot color. It is

146

pretty on them, but they seldom choose it because it has a very soft feeling. When they do choose it, they are likely to choose one with more orange in it.

On the orange card, the Autumn melon color appears as Spring's orange. In the subjective color test, most every Autumn will prefer the bright orange over the softer melon color.

AUTUMN

Fun and Sun

Orange
Gold
Turquoise
Off-white
Browns
Pastel Autumn colors combined with more vivid hues

Business

Browns
Greens
Gold
Off-white with any Autumn color

Touches of orange
Turquoise
Rust

Solemn Occasions

Browns with small touches of brighter colors
Off-white
Rust
Navy blue with small bits of orange or off-white

Romance

Violet
Red-orange
Light olive green
Turquoise in a soft hue

AUTUMN'S COLOR SURROUNDINGS

We often find Autumn individuals who really feel comfortable in the outdoor surroundings where every color of nature reflects their Season. God's own color schemes in the fall of the year are equally as lovely as those blended colors of Autumn that we find in Autumn people's homes.

There is a warm friendliness to the color bouquet, and so Autumns are very happy with the color schemes that have been used for many years in home decorating.

All of us have certain wood tones that are compatible to our Seasons, but Autumns seem to be more prevalent.

I once helped one of my married children move into a home where two Autumn people had lived. All of the walls in the home were (to me) an ugly avacado green. The rugs were in gold in very muted tones and the kitchen colors were dark olive green. These Autumns had been very happy in this house which had been color decorated this way for years. My Winter daughter did not find it so tasteful. If she had been obliged to live in that kind of color environment for long, it would have had a depressing effect on her.

THE EFFECT OF COLOR ON SUMMERS

Taken on a one by one basis, the Summer individual will generally chose his/her own colors. Then looking at the Summer color bouquet in retrospect to the other three Seasons' complete colors, the Summer person often rejects his/her colors. More often the Summer man will accept it, but the woman can see how colorless her bouquet seems to be.

By far, light blue stands out as a favorite color choice for Summer. Most of them have blue eyes, and this is a very complimentary color for them. They feel comfortable in it as it is a quiet, understated color. Gray is another favorite of Summers, especially men.

Summer's red is a quiet rose-blue red, but to a Summer person it seems fire engine bright. The more muted it is, the better they like — more in the magenta range. Summers will dare to wear bright red from another color bouquet as long as they can use white and navy blue with it. Those two supporting tones provide a solid basis for the red, and take away from the severeness of it. When these three colors are used together, it gives a soft effect to those who look at it, hence it is good for Summers.

Very light turquoise is well accepted by Summer and very becoming on those with all shades of hair. Turquoise eyeshadow should not be worn with it as it takes away from the natural light blue of a Summer's eyes.

Gray-brown is another color overlooked by Summer, I think because it is so seldom found in the market. Most light browns are in Spring or Autumn tones. Most Summers have been used to wearing caramels which throw a yellow cast on their already pale skin tone.

Hardly any comment is made when I drape with the pastel green — I find it interesting that a lot of Summers really like Winter's dark pine green instead of their own pastel. A pastel of Winter's green is more pleasing to a Summer.

A Summer is open to pale yellow. They will wear it, but they feel very bright in it even though it is just a whisper of a color. Its compliment, light lavendar, is beautiful on them, but here again, it is rejected many times.

Very light peach is liked by Summers. I do not like it as much as other colors, but it is complimentary to blue eyes and with proper cosmetic colors quite acceptable to the Summer skin tone.

Even if I were to give the very heavy or bright colors to a Summer, he/she would not in all probability wear them anyway. They are quiet and conservative — especially with colors. Winter's darker colors can be worn far away from the face and in not too large an area.

Cosmetic colors must be kept light and in keeping with the ice cream colors of Summer. I have seen Summer girls try the dark, elegant, fashionable lipsticks and blushers, but they look cheap and distasteful on the soft feminine Summer complexion.

SUMMER

Fun and Sun

Off-white
Light blue
Yellow
Green
Red, white, and blue
    combinations

Business

Summer brown, combined
    with off-white or pastels
Navy blue or light blue
Light gray

Solemn Occasions

Navy blue

149

Gray
Summer brown with off-white

Romance

Summer's red
Light blues
Lavender

SUMMER'S COLOR SURROUNDINGS

Give a Summer blue, and they will be happy. They need quiet, restful colors for their unhurried lifestyles. They do not work well in jazzed up color surroundings, but can benefit from a little bright color to help them move a little faster when doing jobs that require a little more energy. Summers will be quite comfortable with Winter's colors in the home as long as they remain on the floor or lower areas of the room. No dark painted walls, please.

If the personality blend is with Spring, then Summers might enjoy small touches of bright color around them, but must realize that they cannot handle the severe intensity of that Season's bouquet on their complexion.

EFFECTS OF COLOR ON WINTER PERSONALITIES

Most Winters readily admit to having several things in their wardrobes that are black. They feel right at home in it. Very young girls will choose black to the dismay of mothers who feel the girls are trying to be too dramatic and glamorous. Quite the contrary is true. Black is a most comfortable favorite color for Winter. It is safe and a place to hide.

If black isn't chosen, then often navy blue comes in as a first color choice. Winters truly do not realize that they are not hiding in these dark colors, but stand out like a beacon in them. The color design of Winter is enhanced by dark, simple and elegant apparel.

Most Winters have a lot of white blouses in their closet. Blue is another favorite in clear bright tones. The mistake of purchasing

150

these in pastels might be made as a Winter sometimes feels like a Summer in personality.

Almost every Winter I drape in green makes a remark like this, "I don't look good in green." They are surprised at how nice it is in a dark, green-black tone.

Yellow is the one color Winters reject completely. Although everyone in the group assures them it is lovely on them, they will not generally wear it.

Some Winters have a feeling for either orange or Spring peach. If skin tone is dark olive, a red-orange is not too bad. It is better not to wear the yellow underbased color side in any clothing.

Dark red is nice, but here again not always acceptable to some Winters because it seems too bright for their conservative natures.

Once in a while a very quiet Winter will surprise everyone and dress up in one of her more dramatic colors.

Winter plum (red-violet) is a new adventure to the conservative Winter personality, but once found through color analysis, it becomes a standby and can be worn in softer hues. It becomes one of Winter's pastels. Mid-tone pink or salmon is very soft and pretty for Winters. Here again, this is a color most do not think of wearing. If Winters would wear their yellow, then this would give three more soft and feminine choices that are effective to use in certain situations. Let me explain.

One would naturally think that Winter colors that are dark would be unnoticeable because they are dark and not as bright as Spring's bright tones. But in reality, black makes the biggest color statement of all with white a close second. If the other Seasons wear these two neutrals, they stand out, but not in a good way. When a truly Winter contrasting person wears them (with elegance and style), then there is nothing that catches the eye more.

In an entire room, a striking Winter will stand out, especially in these colors, or if they are wearing white with any of their other colors.

To themselves they are hiding in conservative hues, but to others they are making a color statement.

Gray is a very good choice for Winter because it looks good, but is also a softer effect if that is what is desired. There are times when it is better to not be so striking in color. The mid-toned pink, yellow and plum are also soft and feminine in feeling.

WINTER

Fun and Sun

Stark white
Black and white prints
Pink
Yellow

Business

Black
Dark gray
Navy blue
Brown
Pine green
White blouses with the above

Solemn Occasions

Brown
Dark grey
Pine green
Navy blue

Romance

Red
Turquoise or blue
Soft or dark plum
Pink
Yellow
Black (for glamorous occasions)
Stark white (for a startling angelic look)

DO THE COLOR BLIND HAVE SUBJECTIVE COLORS?

It was a great surprise to me, during one of my personals for color analysis, to have a lovely client tell me that she had come for her analysis because she is color blind. She had not known of this until she had gone for her physical for entrance to become an airline stewardess.

I said, "Perhaps you are not seriously affected." She told me that the doctors had found her to be extremely blind to color, enough to disqualify her from becoming a stewardess.

I wondered at the time if her subjective color test could even be given with any degree of success, but we proceeded with it anyway and found it to be most interesting.

152

I first asked her if she felt it would benefit her to have her fabric swatches to match for colors. She assured me that if she had a certain color to match to another, she felt she could come up with the same hue.

It had been a shock to her to find out she was color blind because she had really never known that she was, nor had she had any embarrassing thing happen to her — like wearing a mistoned skirt with a strange color blouse.

We proceeded with our eight card color test. She made her choices and these were the findings. By the way, her eye pattern and skin tone revealed later that she was a definite Winter.

Of the colors she chose, six out of eight were Winter colors. This woman, though blind to color, knew her own subjective colors. She did not see them as you and I do, but they were hers and she knew it.

The color analysis for this person was extremely helpful. Not only was she more beautiful in some new found colors and her cosmetics, but she went out of my studio assured that even though she was color blind to colors as the rest of us see them, she saw them in her own way, but correctly for herself.

FINDING THE MOST EFFECTIVE COLORS FOR ALL SEASONS

You would do well to go through your color bouquet and decide which of your colors effect you in different ways. Then go through them and decide the effect they would have on others. The following charts will help you think this out.

COLORS THAT EFFECT ME

Which of my colors make me feel most happy? _____

_____

_____

Which of my colors do I receive the least compliments on?

_____

Which of my colors do I like best?   _____

HOW MY COLORS AFFECT OTHERS

Which of my colors would I wear for a job interview?

_____

_____

Which of my colors would I wear to meet a future mate in?

_____

Which of my colors would I wear to a dance to be the belle of the ball?

_____

Which of my colors would I wear to meet my in-laws to be?

_____

Which of my colors would I wear to help others recognize my nice personality and friendliness?

_____

Which of my colors would impress others the most?

_____

THE COOL AND WARM OF OUR COLOR BOUQUETS

You will remember me talking about the warm and cool colors of the color wheel. These colors give feelings of warmth or of coolness to us and to others. We need to realize which of our colors in our bouquet fit into warm and those that are considered cool. We can use them effectively for ourselves. On the days that

Which of my colors make me feel restful? _____

_____

_____

Which colors do I feel I am romantic in? _____

_____

_____

Which of my colors do I feel are most complimentary? _____

_____

_____

_____

Which of my colors hide my flaws? _____

_____

_____

_____

Which of my colors make my face more attractive? _____

_____

_____

my hair? _____

my eyes? _____

155

we feel a need for a color lift, we can dress in something warm (in color that is). In situations where a more subdued color is called for, a cool color would be just the ticket.

If we want people to warm up to us, we wear our warm colors. If we want to be more businesslike or subdued, the cool tones will be better.

The following charts will help you recognize the warms and cools of your color bouquet.

SUMMER BOUQUET

Yellow - warm
Blue - cool
Lavender - cool
Pastel red-violet -
   warmer, but still cool
Greens - cool, but
   warmer than blue
Pink - warm
Off white - neutral (gives
   no feeling, serves as a
   base for other color)
Gray - neutral
Peach - warm
Brown - neutral with
   with some warmth
Red, white and blue -
   cool
Red - warm
Navy blue - neutral, cool

WINTER BOUQUET

Yellow - warm
Salmon pink - warm
Red-violet - warm
Dark plum - warm, but

156

cooler

White - not a neutral for
Winter. Gives a startling
 cool effect.

Gray - neutral, no color
 effect

Black - not a neutral,
 startling in effect. Warm
 on hot days.

Navy blue - cool, but
 with a softness

Turquoise - cool with
 some warmth

Blue - cool

Dark Turquoise- cool

Pine green - cool

Red - warm

Plum - cool with some
 warmth

Maroon - cool, but with
 some warmth

Brown - neutral, but
 somewhat startling as it
 gets darker.

SPRING BOUQUET

Yellow - warm

Gold - warm

Caramel brown - neutral
 but warm

Yellow-brown - neutral,
 but warm

Rust - warm

Off-white - neutral, no
 color effect

Peach - warm

Darker peach - warm
Hot pink - warm
Red - warm
Periwinkle blue - cool
Yellow-green - very
   warm
Green - warm
Turquoise - cool with
   some warmth
Royal blue - cool
Navy blue - neutral and
   cool

AUTUMN BOUQUET

Gold - warm
Darker gold - warm
Orange - warm
Red-orange - warm
Off-white - neutral, no
   color effect
Caramel - warm
Warm brown - wram
Rust - warm
Olive green, light - cool,
   but still warm
Medium and dark olive
   green - cool with
   some warmth
Kelly green - cool, but
   some warmth
Violet - cool
Turquoise - cool
Navy blue - cool

The principle of using warm and cool colors is fairly simple. Used with logic, it can help you decide what to wear and when.

The interior decorating principles of warm and cool are discussed in the booklet on that subject.

Let us say it is a warm day and you cannot decide what to wear. Look at your warm and cool chart. Would you wear a complete red dress on a very hot day? I hope not, because you will feel warmer in it yourself and others who see you in it will feel that way too. A yellow dress would be alright because the color itself is lighter in tone, and even though it is a warm color, it will stand the effects of the sun. Any of your warm colors can be worn on warm days if used with a greater area of a neutral color. White or off-white is especially good even with red.

RULE FOR LIGHT AND DARK COLORS

Very light colors repel the sun's rays, even though they are warm. If they are light, they are all right for summertime wear.

Very dark colors absorb the sun's rays. You will feel warmer in them even if they are not a warm color. Neutrals in dark tones can be very warm in hot weather.

People's feelings are affected by the cool and warm tones also. The lighter the colors, the less intensely the feelings are stirred. Spring's brights are moving colors. One can overuse the brights though we enjoy them very much.

People around us can be turned on or off to us by the colors we wear. If you know the Season of the person you are wanting to impress, you will understand their conservatism or need for brighter colors or quieter colors.

Spring people will often try to get their mates to dress more brightly, while Summer and Autumn individuals will try for conservatism. Winters might encourage a more dramatic look.

Opposites can attract also. A Spring might be attracted to the Autumn color side or be intrigued with either the Winter or Summer side of the color spectrum.

THE USE OF COLOR IN MENTAL DISTURBANCES

It appears to me that those who are in deep mental depressions turn to the darker colors of Winter or the neutrals of their bouquet. When they are on the mend, they return to their own color bouquet, and the colors can actually help them pull out of their problems.

I have no basis to report on medical problems and color, only those things that have been told to me by my clients. Some have told me that they retreated into dark colors for a time and emerged later when they began to improve mentally.

Winter individuals feel cheerful and calm in the dark colors, and so are not considered abnormal when they wear their own subjective color bouquet.

The blues and reds have been tested in regards to mental patients. Red excites, and blue is a calming influence. Blue acts as a tanquillizer to young infants who are put under a blue light.

Color breathing is practiced by some who feel that it is beneficial to different parts of the body. By placing an amber glass in front of a spectrum of light and letting the resulting yellow colored light strike on the forehead is said by some to relieve sinus problems. Different colored lights are beneficial, they say, to different portions of the body.

The body is said to have its own aura (colored light) coming from it. Some people claim to be able to see it under certain circumstances.

All of these things may be so, but I do not have enough experience in them to recommend or refute them.

What I do know about color is that it is tremendously more important to our lives than most people imagine. It is contained in the life giving light that surrounds us, and is necessary to our well-being and health.

I would not discredit in any way the work done on color psychology thus far by such noted persons as Luscher or Birren. It is my opinion, however, that in numerous years of testing people with color and personality, I find quite a different way to help people recognize their positive and negative personality resources.

The human eye pattern and skin tone color will tell you more about your inherited characteristics and the ways you will react to different situations than any color testing thus devised.

Bibliography

The Luscher Color Test, by Dr. Max Luscher Pocket Books (New York: Random House).

Color In Your World, by Faber Birren New York: (Collier Books, MacMillan Publishing).

Light and Color, by Clarence Rainwater New York: Golden Press (A Golden Science Guide). *Excellent source.

The Art of Color, by Johannes Itten Van Nostrand Reinhold, New York. *excellent source

The Elements of Color, by Itten *Excellent source

Health, Youth and Beauty Through Color Breathing, by Linda Clark-Yvonne Martinne, (Millbrae, California: Celestial Arts).

INTERIOR DESIGN FOR YOU
AND YOUR SEASON

I wonder if you are perhaps like myself. My house just evolved from early marriage to today. Our furniture is now so old that I am beginning to want to keep it because it is rather antique. Much of it is at least over fifty years old because it belonged to family and relatives who handed it down to me.

Nothing in my house really matches, but somehow it feels like home. As I replace items, I will hand them down to my children who have a need for this or that. A few things I will keep because they are too cherished to give away. Probably most everyone has the same situation. Very few people really can ever completely redecorate their homes or start from scratch on a new house and furnish it from corner to corner with everything new.

One of the finest compliments I ever received about my home came from a young friend who, plopping herself down in our old rocker, said, "I just love your house! It feels like home."

A person can't do any better than that, so with the knowledge that my house qualifies as a real home, I set about to instruct you in a subject that I have had no formal training in.

One thing might be said about me and that is, "She certainly knows color." I think I can help you know color too, as it concerns your home and family and their Seasons.

Changing your home atmosphere to more closely match yours and your family's color designs can be as simple as purchasing a few buckets of the right color of paint.

Color in paint, curtains, rugs, accents and accessories can help you feel better about your home and your furniture that is so costly to replace.

The first and most important step to decorating your home for your family is to find out their Seasons as you have found

163

yours.

For that I will refer you to my original text, **Color Me A Season**, to study out and determine the personalities and color design of your family members.

You might be fortunate enough to have a **Color Me A Season** representative near you who can actually do a color analysis for you, if you find that you want to do it that way.

You and your family already have certain preferences that are probably showing your Seasons.

Before I even knew anything about being a Winter individual I was doing a typical Winter paint job in my own home.

My husband, a very agreeable Summer, has certainly put up with some strange color creations in our home. Since he isn't one to paint indoors for me, then I get to pick the color of paint I want. I have, in the past painted my kitchen cupboards a very dark red with white trim, the bedroom walls a dark blue.

In the living room of this same house I did a wall mural of birds painted behind my couch. I won't say it was attractive, but it certainly was different.

One of our living rooms went from a light beige, the color it was when we moved in, to a very dark tangerine red. I loved it. We had it that way for about three years and then I painted the walls stark white, with another mural. This time a paint by number, rather than an original, of a Japanese garden scene in orange and black. To make it more elegant, I glued gold sparkle in touches on the trees and flowers.

A beautifully shaped tree branch was painted white and adorned with snow balls made from clear plastic. This stood in front of a picture window and it certainly was a conversation piece if nothing else.

At one time I dared to plant a lot of plants in our baby bassinet and put it in front of the window. We had a family doctor who made house calls now and then to our home. When he saw this he laughed and assured me that this was a sure way to get a new baby. Sure enough, his prediction came true. The baby bassinet came down to be replaced by other different and daring decorating schemes.

164

As our family grew, we built on to our small home by moving in a huge building and attaching it to the back of our house. Luckily it fit in very well and we almost doubled the space in our home.

The living room furniture moved to the back of the house to fill up a tremendous family room. We purchased some antique railroad benches with wrought iron arms that were about fifteen feet long. We sawed these in appropriate lengths and created four useful pieces of furniture. I painted them black and covered the slats with form rubber padding and tacked on zebra upholstery fabric with brass tacks.

These looked beautiful in the white living room, which had become our parlor because the family did everything in the recreation (family) room.

Our black Zebra benches were the rage even though they didn't set very well for long visits.

Can you see the Winter dramatic choices coming out in me? I certainly could after I learned my Season. I began to understand why I was always doing something dramatically different instead of staying just quiet and more neutral in my home.

Strangely enough, knowing my Season has helped me take on a more refined touch in my color choices, especially since I now understand the feelings and effects of color.

If I had the opportunity, I doubt that I would decorate my home in a complete Winter look. I realize that even though I would be terribly comfortable in my surroundings, there are others in my family that need to be considered.

It may even be possible that I would incorporate some of Spring's color bouquet in more cheerful areas, since that is my other personality blend.*

I hope you are one of the few fortunate persons who has enough money to do just anything you want with your home with no cost counted. But I am afraid that you will be just like the rest of the majority, with not enough money to meet your wants. Let's proceed with that idea in mind.

*See "Understanding Yourself and Others Through Season Analysis" by Bernice Kentner.

Remember, the first step is to find the Seasons of your family and then begin to evaluate how each of you fit in with each other's likes and dislikes. Do you have some mutual likes that you can all agree on? Are there certain types of furniture or certain colors that are entirely distasteful to some members of the family? Who in the family should have the final say or choice concerning the home surroundings? How much are you going to give in to your children's choices? Are you creating an atmosphere for them that will keep them at home because they are comfortable? Are you forcing your children to their friend's homes because yours is too cool or too formal in atmosphere?

These are but a few of the questions one should ask before proceeding further on a decorating project.

EXPLORING YOUR FAMILY'S COLOR BOUQUETS

Since our Seasons depend on inheritance, we are subject to the regular laws of genetics. Both you and your mate may be the same Season and come up with children of different Seasons — my own case being Winter wife, Summer husband; one Winter, two Summers, two Springs as children.

Obviously, we as a family are going to have some color differences. One color that we all can agree on as a negative one is Autumn Olive green.

There are some shades of blues that all of us like and could be happy with. As long as we follow some rules of color theory, we as a family can find some pleasing combinations for our home.

We had a family home evening to find out more about each other's feelings about color. From the subjective color test cards that I use for testing clients, we explored each other's color bouquets. The following might be a fun evening for you and provide you with more insight into the personalities of your individual family members.

TESTING YOUR FAMILY FOR SUBJECTIVE COLORS

Using the fabric swatches for each Season, or the colors from

166

the back of the **Color Me A Season** book, or the color fans for the Seasons, prepare cards by taping or pasting the colors in the following manner on eight separate color cards.

	COLUMN I Summer's:	COLUMN II Winter's:	COLUMN III Spring's:	COLUMN IV Autumn's:
Card 1	Bluish red	Dark red	Bright red	Red-orange
Card 2	Pastel blue	Dark blue	Royal blue	Teal blue
Card 3	Pastel yellow	Medium yellow	Bright yellow	Gold
Card 4	Pastel peach	Dark salmon	Melon or peach	Orange
Card 5	Pastel green	Dark green	Yellow-green	Olive-green
Card 6	Lavender	Red-violet	Periwinkle purple	Violet
Card 7	Light Gray-brown	Dark brown	Yellow-brown	Warm brown
Card 8	Light Turquoise	Dark Turquoise	Medium Turquoise	Teal blue

On cards that you pass out to the family, do not let them know which colors belong to which Season. Show each card and have them mark the one they prefer. After the testing, you can tell them that Column I is Summer, II is Winter, III is Spring, and IV is Autumn.

The following chart may be helpful to you in doing this family activity.

SUBJECTIVE COLOR TEST

Try to clear your mind of all preconceived ideas you may already have about the colors in this test.

Do not think about the colors as those you would wear. Imagine you are coloring a lovely picture or Easter eggs.

Choose the one color off the card that you most like and feel drawn to.

Do not let other people's opinions in the room influence your color choice. There are no right or wrong colors. All are acceptable.

MARK ONLY ONE COLOR

If you must choose another, make it second choice.

COLOR	NUMBER ONE	NUMBER TWO	NUMBER THREE	NUMBER FOUR
RED				
BLUE				
YELLOW				
ORANGE				
GREEN				
PURPLE				
BROWN				
TURQUOISE				

Which of all the eight colors is your favorite? _____

Which is your least favorite?_____

After viewing the entire color bouquet for each of the four Seasons, which one do you like the most? _____

What is your actual Season? _____

Compare as a family each color. Talk about each person's color choices. Discuss the reasons a certain color is disliked. Keep track of colors that the whole family can agree upon.

It might be a good idea to keep this information in a spiral notebook because you will find it very helpful to you, not only for decorating your house, but also for gift choices for Christmas and gift occasions.

Talk about colors and the feeling your children get when they see each color. Personalities will begin to come forth. If you have the booklet *Understanding Yourself and Your Family Through Season Analysis*, you will find it helpful in seeing the personality blends showing up with the color choices.

Ask your family the following questions:

What color carpets would you like in our house?

What should we paint the walls? (Take each room and discuss.)

What color would you like our couch and chairs in the living room?

What colors would you like in your bedrooms?

How can we make our family room compatible to all of us?

If you are a family of mixed Seasons, you may find you have started an uproar. At some point, you, the family decorator, will have to make the final decisions on changes to be made. Children should be heard, but they should not influence you to the extent that you give in to a completely different atmosphere than you would have chosen.

I think all children, within reason, should be given free reign in designing their rooms and choosing the colors they like.

If you are a family that is on the move a lot and may need to sell your home, then walls should be done in more neutral colors so that at the time of selling, the house will more likely fit the buyer.

Let me give you an example. Recently we were doing some

house shopping. We found a home that had the perfect floor plan for our family and our activities. The colors in the home, however, were a complete turn-off to our entire family. Each of the bedrooms was done in unusual wallpaper. One had racing cars, another a bold plaid with stop signs on the other wall, the third a dark plaid again in a very masculine design.

We have girls left at home, so obviously if we had purchased that home we would have had to redo the bedrooms plus some of the other rooms.

Perhaps that family did not plan to sell their home when they decorated it. They made some costly mistakes because it will take a very unusual family to fit into that type of home interior.

Obviously the family members had done their own choosing in decorating their rooms. I am sure they just loved them. What could this family have done to make their house more saleable and yet keep it within the color choice of the individuals living there?

As a general rule, it is better to keep walls the lightest color in the room. Next should be the carpet. Furniture and bedspreads can be darker. The brightest colors in the room should be small touches of color accents in pillows, lamps, accessories.

The young man whose room was decorated in a dark green plaid wall paper with dark red, yellow and green stop signs on the other wall could have had the same effect in his room with the following:

Walls in the room could have been a bone white (suitable for all Seasons); carpet a mid-green. The bedspread would have been very nice in a dark green and rust plaid with two bright red-rust throw pillows on the bed. The same stop sign wall paper could be pasted onto a large 3' x 5' cardboard, framed and hung over the dresser or head of the bed. The wastepaper basket could also be covered with the paper, as could a few plant holders. Car models could adorn shelves on the wall with driving paraphenalia, etc. Stop sign draperies could also be made, or better yet, a plain pair of bone white draperies would make the room seem larger.

We now have achieved the same effect in the first room but its look can be taken with the occupant when he moves to another

170

house.

I could have moved right into a bedroom like that with bone white walls and green rug. I could have made it seem very Wintery, or Springy, or even Summery. It might have sold us the house instead of discouraging us from buying.

EVALUATION OF YOUR HOME DECOR

Probably the best place to start is going through your home room by room with an air of inspection to determine the colors of each room.

Using your copy of **Color Me A Season**, with the four color bouquets, or the fabric swatch packets, or the single or professional color fans, start in the entry of your home at the front door.

As you open the door, examine the color of the entryway carpet. Which Season's color is it? Go on to the walls or wall paper. Fill in the blanks of the following charts to make your home evaluation.

You may be amazed at some of the color combinations that are in your home. It will help you to see why some things are not very pleasing. Perhaps you have an Autumn brown with a Winter color.

Knowing about the two color sides can be a very useful bit of information and can save you from making wrong color choices. From the **Color Me A Season** color fans, the Summer and Winter colors are quiet and blue underbased; the Autumn and Spring colors are warmer and yellow undertoned.

It is possible to put the corresponding Season's colors together, but when you try to mix, or go across to the other color side, then the colors will fight each other rather than blend.

Do your home color evaluation during the day, if possible, so the colors will be true in daylight. It will be more difficult for you to do this under any other kind of lighting.

Walls _____
                        Season   Color

Wall accessories_____
                        Season   Color

_____
                        Season   Color

_____
                        Season   Color

Metals _____
                   Metal Color   Season

Furniture_____
              Wood color   Season   Item

_____
              Wood color   Season   Item

_____
              Wood color   Season   Item

_____
              Wood color   Season   Item

Fabric on furniture_____
                   Season's type   Item

_____
                   Season's type   Item

_____
                   Season's type   Item

Fabric types:

Small floral: Summer

Paisley or plaids: Autumn

Bright prints and florals: Spring

Geometrics, stripes: Winter

172

HOME COLOR EVALUATION CHART

Fill in the following spaces with the Season the color belongs to.

Entry Hall carpet _____
                          Season   Color
Entry Hall walls or wallpaper _____
                                    Season   Color

Entry Hall wall accessories _____
                                  Season   Color

if metal_____
                    Gold   Silver
              (Spring-Autumn)   (Summer-Winter)

Entry Hall furniture _____
                            Wood type   Fabric type

Season's feelings that the hallway gives _____

Furniture types:

Dark and heavy, modern contemporary: Winter

Blonde, light delicate details: Summer

Warm browns, sturdy, simple: Autumn

Warm browns, early American, natural: Spring

Things I need to change _____

_____

_____

LIVING ROOM

Carpet _____
                          Season   Color

Room Accessories   _____   _____
                            Season   Color

(pillows, bric-a-
brac, etc.)   _____   _____
                            Season   Color

                    _____   _____
                            Season   Color

The Season's look or Season's blend I am trying to achieve: __

_____

Things I need to change to achieve this _____

_____

_____

FAMILY ROOM

Carpet_____
                            Season   Color

Walls _____
                            Season   Color

Wallpaper or secondary wall _____
                            Season   Color

Wall accessories_____
                            Season   Color

_____
                            Season   Color

_____
                            Season   Color

Metals _____
                      Metal Color   Color

Furniture_____
            Wood color   Season   Item

174

	Wood color	Season	Item

	Wood color	Season	Item

Fabrics on furniture _____

	Season	Color	Item

Room Accessories_____

	Season	Color	Item

	Season	Color	Item

	Season	Color	Item

The Season or Seasons' blend I am trying to achieve _____

_____

Things I need to change _____

_____

_____

KITCHEN

Floors _____

                            Season   Color

Walls _____

                            Season   Color

Wallpaper or secondary wall _____

                            Season   Color

Appliances _____

	Color	Season	Item

	Color	Season	Item

Cupboards _____
                    Wood or metal   Season

Kitchen furniture _____
                        Color   Season   Item

_____
                        Color   Season   Item

The Season or Season's blend I am trying to achieve _____

_____

Things I need to change _____

_____

_____

_____

MASTER BEDROOM

Carpet _____
                              Season   Color

Walls _____
                              Season   Color

Wallpaper _____
                              Season   Color

Furniture _____
                        Color   Season   Item

_____
                        Color   Season   Item

_____
              Metal color   Wood Color   Item

Bedspread _____
                              Season   Color

176

Drapes_____
                        Season   Color

Room Accessories_____
                  Color   Season   Item

_____
                  Color   Season   Item

_____
                  Color   Season   Item

What is the Season or Season type of the occupants of this room?

_____

What do I need to change?_____

_____

_____

_____

_____

BEDROOM 2

Carpet _____
                        Season   Color

Walls _____
                        Season   Color

Wallpaper _____
                        Season   Color

Furniture_____
                  Color   Season   Item

_____
                  Color   Season   Item

	Metal color	Wood Color	Item
Bedspread			

	Season	Color
Drapes		

	Season	Color
Room Accessories		

	Color	Season	Item

	Color	Season	Item

	Color	Season	Item

What is the Season or Season type of the occupants of this room?

_____

What do I need to change? _____

_____

_____

_____

_____

BEDROOM 3

	Season	Color
Carpet		

	Season	Color
Walls		

	Season	Color
Wallpaper		

178

Furniture _____
                    Color   Season   Item

_____
                    Color   Season   Item

_____
           Metal color   Wood Color   Item

Bedspread _____
                              Season   Color

Drapes _____
                              Season   Color

Room Accessories _____
                    Color   Season   Item

_____
                    Color   Season   Item

_____
                    Color   Season   Item

What is the Season or Season type of the occupants of this room?

_____

What do I need to change? _____

_____

_____

_____

_____

BEDROOM 4

Carpet _____
                              Season   Color

179

Walls _____
                                     Season   Color

Wallpaper _____
                                       Season   Color

Furniture_____
                        Color   Season   Item

_____
                        Color   Season   Item

_____
               Metal color   Wood Color   Item

Bedspread _____
                                       Season   Color

Drapes_____
                                     Season   Color

Room Accessories_____
                        Color   Season   Item

_____
                        Color   Season   Item

_____
                        Color   Season   Item

What is the Season or Season type of the occupants of this room?

_____

What do I need to change?_____

_____

_____

_____

_____

LAUNDRY ROOM

Floor_____
                             Season   Color

Walls _____
                             Season   Color

Appliances _____
                Color   Season   Item

_____
                Color   Season   Item

What do I need to change?_____

_____

OUTSIDE OF HOUSE

Color of House _____
                             Season   Color

Trim_____
                             Season   Color

Flowers and Shrubs _____
                             Season   Color

_____
                             Season   Color

_____
                             Season   Color

From its appearance, this house looks like a family of _____

_____ lives here.
     Season

What I need to change_____

_____

181

The overall feeling of my home is _____
                                                    Season
I want it to be_____
Winter—Elegant, rich
Summer—Quiet, restful
Spring—Bright, cheerful
Autumn— Warm, friendly

When you have completed this evaluation of your home, you will have a very useful tool to make some changes. Perhaps you found your decor perfect for you and your family.

Most will have a few tiny alterations, however, and I hope the following hints about the looks for the Seasons will help you.

I cannot stress too much that *You* are You and will have definite feelings about colors and furniture, etc. If you find that the suggestions for the Seasons are not pleasing to you, then by all means use those that you like.

It is ridiculous to follow instructions that don't fit you. If you are open to suggestion, then perhaps you can spend some time shopping around and looking at the different furniture items, etc., to get a feel of the things you feel comfortable with.

Oftentimes our Season's blend comes through in what we like. I, as a Winter with some Spring in my temperament, can be happy in either a Winter decor or one with some of Spring's colors. I really do, however, feel more comfortable and at home in my own Winter environment. Since my family does not share the same Season, we can agree on some other colors that are pleasing to all of us.

I do try to keep the overall look of a room in either the blue undersided colors or the gold based tones. I try not to mix those two in any one room. The effect is much more pleasing to everyone.

You will see what I mean. Just notice after your color evaluation of your home how much more pleasing the rooms are that are completely in the blue undertone or gold undertone hues. Even though your Season may be on the other side, you will not object so much to a room that has been properly color-coded as to one that has colors that fight one another.

182

STAYING ON THE CORRECT COLOR SIDE

We had to replace a bathroom floor recently due to water leakage. The adjacent hall carpet was in a turquoise blue, more on the key side of the warm Autumn shade. The bathroom walls are painted in a yellow-based Spring pink. The question was, "What kind of floor can we put in this bathroom that will save us from painting the walls? I certainly didn't want to have to do a complete new decorating scheme on the bathroom, because the paint was in very good condition.

With my knowledge about the two sides of color, I decided that the walls were warm enough in the yellow-based pink, and that a very good color for the floor would either be a neutral brown or tan (which didn't strike me as being good with pink) or search for a yellow based blue.

I was elated. The very first tile shop that we visited had a tile pattern in Autumn's steel blue. This is a light blue that has a rather gray cast to it. It is beautiful on Autumns, and blends with other Autumn colors.

We purchased the tile and brought it home and laid it on the floor. It is absolutely beautiful. It blends with Spring's pink very well and with the adjacent hall rug. The eye goes from one color to another without any shock. It is a total look and very well coordinated with the room and other rooms that can be seen from it.

With the professional "Color Me A Season" color fan you will be able to color coordinate your home also. Just remember that Summer and Winter colors blend together and that Spring and Autumn match.

In color analysis for individuals, it is important to wear only your own colors with the exception of using a little bit of your corresponding Season for touches or basics to wear brighter colors with.

In your home it is another thing. You may choose colors completely from the Summer-Winter side to decorate with, as with Autumn-Spring.

This is one way that you can please persons in your family who are of a different Season than yourself as long as they are your corresponding Season on the same color side.

USING THE COLOR ME A SEASON FANS
TO PURCHASE PAINTS

The **Color Me a Season** fans no longer come in a professional size. They have been added to and come in plastic covers for each fan; if you want to use them for interior decorating purposes, you will need to order all four fans.

Remember, the Summer and Winter fans are the cool side; Autumn and Spring, the warm. These fans are custom made for us and do not have paint mixing notations on each of the cards that are not Bouquet Colors.

These paint colors are standard throughout the paint industry and most companies will have colors of paint that you can match your desired color to.

COLOR ME A SEASON Educational Color Corp. (P.O. Box 864, Concord, California 94519) will be glad to send you product sheets and any information that will help you better understand color.

It is most important in any type of decorating to understand the ways you can use color.

From **Color Me A Season** I repeat this information:

UNDERSTANDING THE DIFFERENT COLOR SCHEMES
COLOR COMBINATIONS

Monochromatic. One color is used in various tints and shades, some bright and some dull. Summers keep majority of tones light. Use some dark to add interest and contrast. All other Seasons keep majority of tones in pure hues from your bouquet (of sixteen colors) or from the end colors on your color fans, using lighter tints of color to add interest and contrast. This is where your color fans will be so helpful to you.

Analogous. Colors that lie next to each other on the color wheel (related), including their tints and shades. All Seasons should vary shades and tints to add interest and variety. Winters remember to keep your color schemes simple. Summers, here again, use a majority of tints rather than darker shades.

Complimentary. Complimentary uses colors that are opposite on the color wheel. For instance, orange and blue. Orange, the warm color and blue, the cool. Summers and Winters, use the majority of cool colors and Springs and Autumns use a larger amount of the warm.

VARYING THE COOLS AND THE WARMS

Complimentary color schemes are very pleasing in rooms of your home because of the interest of using cool colors with warm.

You will find that all the color's compliments are the opposite in warm or cool. This is pleasing to the eye and helps to balance out the feeling in a room.

You could choose to do a room in entirely warm colors. For example, let's say red-orange and its analogous colors red and orange. The neutral wall would be a creamy yellow-beige. All colors in the room would be varying tints of red, orange, and red-orange. After a time one would begin to feel the heat of these colors and become uncomfortable in the room. If some of the complimentary color blue would be used in the rug or pillows or lamps, then the eye could rest on these to give relief from the entire warmth of this analogous color scheme.

It is pleasing to use either an analogous or monochromatic color scheme and then add to it a complimentary touch of some of the colors that lie across from the shades or tints you have used to add interest and balance to your room.

ADDING INTEREST AND TEXTURE TO YOUR DECOR

No matter what your Season is, to make a room interesting, you need to add some elements of different textures. This is achieved by having some wood, some upholstery, some metal and some fabric.

Just imagine how uninteresting a room would be if per-chance it had wood floors, panelling on the walls and all wood furniture.

Our pioneer ancestors tried to add interest to their humble abodes by hanging curtains and crocheting or knitting doilies, etc., to add to the room to soften it and make it more homey.

One woman who had no material to spare, used sheets of a newspaper she had saved and cut out lace patterns and then hung

186

them in the windows of her mud adobe dwelling to simulate curtains.

Rugs were made of rags by braiding them and sewing them together in rounds or oval shapes to cover dirt floors.

Women today delight in making crafty things to brighten up their homes. These things are invaluable. They add bits and pieces of your personality. You will be choosing things that you like to do and which are likely to be in your Season.

I happened upon a print of a Winter Spanish lady clothed in her black lace mantilla. There is nothing beautiful or fetching about the picture, but it really appealed to me and so I framed it to hang in my bedroom. I used a frame with a glass that I already had at home and the print did not fit it exactly. To remedy that, I purchased a large piece of pure red poster board as a picture mate and centered the print on that and then put it in the frame. To me it is quite striking and I really like it.

My husband (who likes red) likes it also and so it fits in our room very well.

I will attempt to outline now the different Season's colors and looks for your home. You may disagree with me completely, but at least it will give you some basis for a start.

Let me give you a word of caution about hiring a home decorator who doesn't understand your personality type.

It is rather like designing clothing. The designer designs clothing that fits his/her Season type. Unless they are very universal in their knowledge of the four areas of fashion, they are likely to work best in materials and styles that are from their own personality area.

Home designers could benefit, as could fashion designers, by learning more about our methods of Season analysis and incorporating it into their work.

Johannes Itten in "The Art of Color" (New York: Van Nostrand Reinhold, 1973), points out that there are three types of people when it comes to color.

1. Epigoni: Those who have no knowledge of their own colors. They copy others or follow the instruction of other people.

2. Originals: Those who know their own colors and expect other people to use them also, even though they are not right for the other person.
3. Universalists: Individuals who comprehend the entire color circle (all Season's colors) and allow others to use colors that are best for them.

You can see the effect it would have on the work of a designer or decorator if they fit into these three categories. Hopefully, you can find a Universalist to help you with your clothing or your home decor.

Unfortunately, we find different designers who do their own Season's look in everything they do.

It isn't necessary that they remain in this color knowledge category. They may become more universal in color and should strive to do so as they learn about Season analysis.

STARTING FROM THE FLOOR UP

Types of carpet that will be appealing to the Seasons: This is the largest unbroken area of color in a room, and so it must be chosen wisely for you and your Season.

SUMMER

Summers may prefer soft, velvety textures. The carpet may be shaded in a monochromatic color scheme in soft shades. A rug with very detailed pattern would also be enjoyable.

BEST COLORS FOR SUMMER CARPET

> Off-white
> Cream beige
> Soft gray-brown
> Magenta
> Mint green
> Baby blue
> Medium blue

Navy blue
Soft gray

WINTER

Winters may prefer elegant carpets with deep textures, con-trasting patterns and colors, dark and dramatic color.

BEST COLORS FOR WINTER CARPET

Dark brown
Dark green
White (not practical, but gorgeous)
Pure dark blue
Pure dark red
Maroon
Medium blue-based pink
Medium gray
Medium yellow

SPRING

Springs may prefer natural, crisp carpets with an ease of care quality; two toned or patterned will be liked.

BEST COLORS FOR SPRING CARPET

Rust
Off-white
Caramel brown
Bright red
Light yellow-green
Yellow-gray
Bright yellow
Melon or peach
Light turquoise

189

AUTUMN

Autumns may prefer carpets in rich earth-toned colors. Textures in sturdy tweeds or heavy shags; Persian or patterned rugs in an overall flowing design.

BEST COLORS FOR AUTUMN CARPET

Light caramel beige
Gold
Orange rust
Warm brown
Dark rust
Melon
Kelly green
Avacado green
Olive green

CARPET AS THE FIRST CHOICE COLOR

A wise decorator will choose the carpet first before even deciding on the color for walls.

Some persons advocate using a much liked picture or piece of drapery material and picking out the basic colors in the print to build a room around. Either way will be fine as long as you realize that the carpet will lend the most color to the room. It most certainly would be an important color choice.

I have a wonderful Spring friend who invited me over to her home to see if she had decorated her living room in a Spring decor. She was afraid, after being color coded into Spring, that her home might be wrong, but she really liked it very much. I paid a visit to her home. Her home is so Springlike and it has all been done by her. She and her Autumn husband both love their living room which is dominated by a beautiful couch and love seat upholstered in a large rust-orange and off-white flowered print.

A prized rug, sent to them by one of their children, graces the middle of the floor laid upon the carpet. The rug has a design with a lot of Spring's royal blue and white. The business of the patterns blend together in a nice combination for a Spring and Autumn family.

Artifacts from their family, who are quite universal in their travels, grace the tables and add to the personality of the room.

Dorothy readily admits that her home is her castle and she has an almost reverent feeling when she sits in her living room.

That is what decorating is all about. It's creating a home atmosphere where you and your family feel safe, secure and warm. Home should be a refuge for the entire family.

COLOR IS MOST IMPORTANT

Your first consideration is to get the correct color in your carpet. If you settle for one that is a wrong color choice you will be dissatisfied with it all the while it is on your floors. Shop around and really look for what you want.

Have a second or third possibility when you look, if you can't find your first choice. You will not want to sacrifice quality for color and so be flexible to some extent.

You may, for instance, have a difficult time finding the right purple for a carpet but yellow or gold might be a second choice with some of the purple you want incorporated into the fabrics used in the room.

Your carpet is one place that you cannot scrimp on quality. It takes more wear and tear than anything else, and so, if you can, get top grade carpeting. That is why you should be a little flexible with the color.

I know you will be able to find a color from your color bouquet that will satisfy you.

CHOOSING THE WALL COLORS

Your next most important color choice will be the wall coloring. This is the next largest area of color and it will either hem you in with color, or give you an open feeling in your room.

In deciding between a warm or cool color from your Season's

bouquet, you need to consider the atmosphere of the room itself.

Rooms that have a great deal of sunshine might need to be cooled down a little with a pastel blue or green, even a lavendar wall. Those that have darkness or a cool feeling, already, would benefit from a warm beige, very light yellow, or gold, etc.

COLORS AND TEMPERATURE

Every Season has both warm and cool colors. Just for general information, the following are warm colors:

Red
Yellow
Orange
Yellow-orange
Red-orange
Yellow-green

The following are midway between cool and warm:

Green
Red-violet

The following are cool colors:

Blue
Blue-violet
Blue-green

Knowing the cool and warm colors from your color bouquet can be very useful to you.

At one time we had a kitchen that had many windows facing the East. It was bright and cheerful — so much so that the yellow that was featured in the room made it seem unbearably hot. I counteracted it by painting all the walls in the room a very light wedgewood blue. White shades were put in the windows with a darker blue fringe and tassles. Along the cabinets I kept a cannister set of blue and white jars and plant holders of blue and white.

The room had a clean look and the color cooled the room down. Though we don't live in that home anymore, we all remember our blue kitchen and hope one day to have another like it.

Keeping the Walls Neutral in Tone

Unless you are really experienced at choosing color and decorating, you cannot go far wrong by using a neutral light tint from your colors.

Neutrals For Summer

Off-white

Very light gray-brown

Light gray

Navy is a neutral, but you should not use it for walls because it is too dark.

Many of the pastels of Summer are so light that they are almost neutral in tone.

Neutrals For Winter

Stark white

Gray

Gray-brown (use it as a light tint)

Summer pastels used in their lightest tints may be used in a Winter room as long as darker hues are featured in the carpet and furniture.

Neutrals For Spring

Off-white

Beige

Caramel browns

Yellow-gray (very light)

Very light pastel tint of Spring gold

Very light pastels of Spring colors

Neutrals For Autumn

Off-white

Beige

Light gold

Caramel browns

Light olive green

As a general rule, if walls are painted in neutral tones or very very light pastels of the color bouquet you are featuring, they will serve as a good background for your furniture and other accessories in the room.

USING DARK COLORS OR WALLPAPER

Occasionally a room or a space in your home calls for more dramatic coverage. Hallways are a good example. Your hall should introduce your guests to your family as they are greeted into the home.

There should either be a wallpaper that expresses:

Winter, elegance
Summer, peaceful
Spring, friendly, joyful
Autumn, warm and inviting

Go to your wallpaper store and study the kinds of paper offered there. Decide what the colors in the paper depict. How do you feel as you look at them? Check the colors with the color bouquets in **Color Me A Season** to see which Season they fit in.

If you are Winter and have painted your room or rooms adjacent to the hallway a stark white, you would not want to put up a wallpaper that had a background of off-white or beige.

The same would hold true if the wall were beige and the paper a different background that did not match.

Wallpapers are just like dress fabric. They have a Season to them and they give off an effect of color and personality. Make sure you get one that follows the rules of the Season you are trying to create an effect for.

NEXT CHOICE, DRAPERY

Window treatment is very important in the room. If the area is small you will be better off using a color that is like the wall coloring so it adds space and openness.

Very colorful drapery belongs in larger rooms. Dark colors will also cut down on the apparent size of the room.

The print on the fabric will also create an atmosphere in the room, as does wallpaper on the walls. Large prints, unless they are very blending, will dominate the room and take attention away from other things in the room.

Sometimes if you have furniture that is not just what you would like it to be, you can hide it with more dramatic color on the walls or in the draperies.

You can use draperies or curtains as a background for tables or furniture that do not do so well by themselves against a neutral wall background.

WHICH FABRIC TO CHOOSE FOR YOUR SEASON

Draperies are made from fabrics that have a long-wearing, sturdy quality. They will not necessarily have the feel of the type of fabric that goes best with the Season's clothing, therefore one should choose a good quality fabric that has the right COLOR for you and the right type of print for your Season.

As a general rule, these types of fabrics will appeal to the Seasons for draperies:

SUMMER: Materials that have a softness to them with a matte finish. Cottons and crushed velvets; some soft woolen fabrics; sheers, used at the window rather than drapery.

Prints in the fabrics: Small detailed prints, flowing floral designs in soft colors, blending fragile designs.

WINTER: Luxurious fabrics are just right for Winters. Satin and velvet, shiny materials, suede and silk. A look of richness and elegance.

Prints in the fabrics: An elegant plainness is satisfying for Winter. It may have a shiny weave or silvery shading. Geometric prints or some checks and plaids appeal to Winter.

SPRING: Crisp fabrics such as linen, chintz, poplin, cotton blends, natural fibers.

Prints in the fabrics: Joyous, fun materials with small designs such as red apples or those that are identifiable as an object. Nature patterns, especially small flowers seen in the springtime.

AUTUMN: Fabrics with a feel. Those with texture and weave. Rough fabrics such as tweeds, rough linen and raw silk. Heavy woolens with a nub or apparent weave to them.

Prints in the fabrics: Overall paisley or abstract designs. Plaids in a heavy nubby fabric. Some may prefer Jungle prints with gold, brown and green surrounding animals of nature. Plain fabric with no print, but a nubby texture.

FURNITURE FOR YOUR SEASON

After the carpet is laid and the walls are painted and the

drapery has been hung, we begin to move in our own personal furniture and belongings to complete the picture in each room.

My furniture, fortunately, is mostly in dark brown tones which is satisfying to me and my Winter Season.

It used to be felt that all woods should match in the room, but now it is more fashionable to have different things that blend together adding that touch of interest or texture to the room.

If all furniture matches completely, then the room seems well-coordinated, but the eye quickly passes over all the articles leaving us no place to linger and look. It is well, therefore, to place a wooden table or wood object here and there that doesn't match the arms of the chairs and end tables, etc.

In arranging furniture in the room, remember this rule: NEVER PLACE TWO WOODEN OBJECTS NEXT TO EACH OTHER. Place a wooden chair next to something that is upholstered for a good effect.

If your home has hard wood floors, don't place all wooden furniture in the room. Either break the wood effect with throw rugs or carpets or use a lot of fabric and upholstery in the room. Otherwise the room will have a cold barren effect.

Wood Types for the Seasons

I will give you some types of wood finishes that will be pleasing to the Seasons, but before I do, consider the four different browns in the color bouquets. Look at each of the browns to see what the color effect is.

SUMMER'S Brown is — Light gray-brown

WINTER'S Brown is — Dark gray-brown

SPRING'S Brown is — Yellow-brown

AUTUMN'S Brown is — Warm orange-brown

If you drape a person in these four browns you can tell their Season as well as with four reds or greens, etc.

Brown is really very different and somewhat difficult to pick out when you shop for it. You might find yourself with the wrong Season's brown unless you match it to your fabric swatch or color fan.

In choosing your wooden furniture and accessories, you can match them to your color of brown to get the feeling right for your Season's room.

In general, the feeling for woods for the Seasons is:

Summer: Quiet, light, non-shiny surfaces, antiqued finishes in very light tones.

Winter: Dark, heavy, wrought iron black or antique white, glass and metal.

Spring: Natural finishes, light, wicker and weaves, warm yellow-brown tones.

Autumn: Warm browns, sturdy, but not heavy, brass or gold.

These are the wood stains by Seasons:

SUMMER

Maple

Rosewood

Blond

Antique (painted)

WINTER

Teak wood

Walnut

Mahogony

Painted (white or black)

198

SPRING

Pine

Oak

Light Walnut

AUTUMN

Redwood

Mahogany (red)

Warm Pine

Cherry

MIXING WOODS IN A ROOM

It stands to reason that for interest's sake, as I said before, you may want to have a little variation of wood in the room. You might try using the different types within your Season, or go over into your corresponding Season and use some of their furniture with yours.

SUMMER-WINTER correspond
AUTUMN-SPRING correspond

Anytime you need to vary your colors, you can use a little of your corresponding Season to add interest and detail. As long as the room is kept in the majority of your look and your colors you will still achieve the Season's effect you are trying to create.

You can see how I, as a Winter, can satisfy both my Summer husband's color taste and mine by placing some colors from both Seasons in the room. By doing so, I break some of the starkness and elegance of Winter enough to make the room more inviting.

A Spring-Autumn combination will benefit from some Autumn colors with bright touches of Spring colors. The room will take on a more serious nature and yet appeal also to a Spring individual.

Spring-Summer combinations can be achieved by using the brights from Spring on a very light pastel background of carpet and walls or perhaps using light blue which is very pleasing to Spring individuals and to Summers.

Spring-Winter combination will be very contrasting, using stark white walls or black furniture upholstery with some of the bright Spring contrasting colors in pillows and pictures in the room.

Summer-Autumns would be satisfied with a light steel (yellow-based) blue as the main color effect in the room, with off-white or beige walls (suitable for both Seasons). Some orange touches would satisfy the Autumn and many plants bringing in the green of Autumn.

Winter-Autumns might like dark brown with lots of green. Walls in an off-white with touches of heavy metals in the room. Turquoise (our universal color) would appeal to both Seasons.

These may break the color key rule of never going into the other contrasting Season's side to combine colors, but if one trys hard enough something can usually be found that will please everyone in the house.

If that is impossible, then you will just have to decorate the room for the person who will spend the most time there OR in the Season's effect you want to give to those visiting you.

Try to get something going for your Season because you will be happier in your surroundings that way.

METAL TYPES FOR THE SEASONS

When it comes to choosing accessories for your room that have metal on them, you should know your metal type.

They are as follows:

Summer

Silver
Rose gold
Pewter

Winter

Silver
Chrome
Platinum or White gold

Spring

Yellow gold
Green gold
Shiny brass

Autumn

Dark gold
Copper
Bronze
Unpolished Brass

Glass is most appropriate for the Winter Season, but may of course be used for others. Some nice Spring effects can be done with glass tables. The difficulty is that most things that are made of glass are used with chrome legs or arms. This is definitely better for Winter.

Most Summers like wood better than the more modern or contemporary look of glass and chrome.

Crystal chandaliers are adored by Winter people. Summers would like them with delicate details, Autumns with brass or gold intermingled. Springs would be the least likely to choose this type of light over their dining table. It doesn't fit the Springs natural or casual feeling.

LAMPS AND ACCESSORIES

Just about all of us have several things that perhaps we would not have chosen for ourselves in our home when it comes to accessories and bric-a-brac. Some of them don't even match our personality but they remind us of those who gave them to us or who left us these things as heirlooms. We should use these for points of interest in our homes.

One family gathered together objects that had meaning for them and placed them on a small table in the entry way to their home. It was an introduction to their family and many a conversation was easily started from the comments as people entered the home.

Your bric-a-brac and momentoes can always be gathered together and placed in an interesting way on shelves on the wall or scattered around the room on the various end tables or coffee tables in the room.

I knew one extremely good *housekeeper* (I use that word on purpose instead of homemaker) whose home was completely sterile of any junk or dust catchers, as she called them. Her house was immaculate and free of litter. I admire that, of course, but I think I would have liked it if she had been a little more human like the rest of us who have a lot of interesting (to us only, maybe) momentoes lying around the house.

Interesting Accessories for the Seasons

SUMMER

Silk flowers, dresden figurines, family pictures in cameo-like frames, soft pillows, embroidered and crocheted afgans in light ice cream colors, tiny animals, birds, candy dishes with delicate flowers on the lids, etc.

WINTER

Crystal glass, mirrors, metal figurines, candle holders (silver or black), marble pieces, animals cut out of rock, sculptures of great musicians, large real silk or real flower arrangements.

SPRING

Straw flowers, baskets, colorful figurines, plants, bright pillows, crewel pictures, macrame hangings, pictures of friends in wooden frames or wall hangings.

AUTUMN

Antique pieces, brass or metal boxes, earthtoned flower arrangements, many plants, wall hangings with homey sayings, sculptures of wood or metal, tweed or textured pillows, brass candle holders and door knockers.

This list could go on and on, but you will catch the feeling we are after. Now just mix a few of these items you already have and you will get your Season's atmosphere in your home.

WHERE TO GET IDEAS

I could print many colorful pictures in this booklet that would help you get some ideas for rooms for the Seasons. That would be fun to do sometime, but in the meantime, why don't you go to the library and look through all the home decorating or house beautiful type magazines. They are resplendent in ideas for decorating.

Look through the pictures and try to decide which Season is featured in each of the rooms in the magazine. You will find that many of them have either colors or furniture or accessories that would be good to copy for your Season.

Often you can get an idea for your home from these magazines that will help you redecorate your home. Sometimes a good idea leads you to something you like better. In searching for a certain fabric pictured in the magazines we might not find that particular one, but run onto another with the same color that we might even like better.

Books on home decorating are great also and will help you very much.

Two booklets that you can purchase are, "A Dictionary of Textile Terms" by Dan River Inc., Greenville, South Carolina. Send your check to Dictionary Dept., Dan River, Inc., 111 West 40th Street, New York, NY 10018. Cost, 50¢

"Seng Furniture Facts" The Seng Company, 1450 N. Dayton St., Chicago, Il 60622. 196 pages of information about furniture and how to use it. Send $1.50.

There were a lot of interesting facts in these booklets that I felt you would like, but a bit too lengthy to include in this one.

Most Ethan Allen Furniture Stores have a beautiful magazine type of catalogue that shows their furniture in room settings. This is usually free if you will go to their store and ask for it. They may charge a little for it in some places. It is very good to get ideas from. This store also offers some classes in decorating in some areas, so check with them on this.

Your local college may have some classes that you can take (on an audit basis) at very low cost to learn more about home decoration.

Adult classes through your community centers sometimes offer instruction in this field also.

There are just a lot of good resources to help you in your home decorating. I have had 25 years of experience in homemaking classes from Relief Society (my church's women's group) that have really given me a good education for making a house into a home.

Check some of your local churches for women's group meetings that teach these homemaking arts to their women.

Another source of information is just talking about and getting together with other people who are building and adding to their home decor. They will have ideas that you can use in your home, too.

HAVE UNIVERSAL IDEAS

I hope that you will be able to adapt a universal approach to decorating for yourself and for other people of a different Season. You may find out that you like this part of Season Analysis so much that you can develop a flair for helping other people decorate their homes for their Seasons.

My particular love is creating beautiful women with cosmetics and clothing colors, but I quite like every phase of Season analysis. I think knowing your Season is one of the most helpful things you can learn. It will affect your entire life when you realize how much color is involved with our inner feelings and our personality output.

I hope this information will be a catalyst to further learning about your Season and how to incorporate it into your home surroundings.

Since the printing of this book Bernice Kentner has created many color aids, plus Workbook and Trade School Education through Color Me A Season Inc. Licensed in California. Be sure to read "A Rainbow in Your Eyes" a textbook for certified color consultants and those interested in their own color design.